APPALACHIAN HERITAGE

VOL. 45, NO. 1
WINTER 2017

EDITOR
Jason Howard

STUDENT ASSISTANTS
Rhea Carter, Emily Masters, Dylan Mullins
& Hannah Musick

MANUSCRIPT READERS
Katherine Scott Crawford, Adam Lambert,
& Patti Frye Meredith

ESTABLISHED IN 1973

PUBLISHED QUARTERLY
by Berea College
CPO 2166
205 N. Main Street
Berea, KY, 40404

www.appalachianheritage.net

©2017 by Berea College. Vol. 45, No. 1, Winter 2017. All rights reserved. No part of this publication may be reproduced without the prior permission of *Appalachian Heritage*. Periodicals postage paid at Berea, Kentucky, and at additional mailing offices. ISSN# 03632318.

The short stories in this publication are works of fiction. Names, characters, places, and incidents are either the products of the authors' imaginations or are used fictitiously. Any resemblance to actual events, locales, or persons, living or dead, is entirely coincidental. The views expressed in the creative nonfiction herein are solely those of the authors.

Electronic submissions only at www.appalachianheritage.net

Distributed by the University of North Carolina Press. Basic subscription price: $30/year for individuals, $60/year for institutions. For subscription requests and inquiries, visit the magazine's website, email uncpress_journals@unc.edu, or call 919.962.4201.

CONTENTS

SPECIAL FEATURE: HUNTING RITES

INTERVIEW

CRAFT ESSAY

BOOK REVIEW

COVER PHOTOGRAPH

Kristian Thacker, *Laura Mae on Church Street, June 2014*

EDITOR'S NOTE

JASON HOWARD

One of the most formative moments of my life was when I acquired a library card. I was around seven, and one day after school my father, a high school history teacher, took me to the squat, brown-bricked building in downtown Pineville, Kentucky. The kind librarian at the desk handed me a form and with my father, I filled in all the relevant information: name, address, telephone number. Then came the most thrilling part—my signature, promising to return all items, accepting responsibility for any damage incurred by them. I felt so grown-up as I penned my full name in the new cursive script I had learned the year before, taking care to stay on the black line that ran underneath. When all the formalities were complete, the librarian handed me the laminated card, which I gave pride of place in my blue canvas-and-Velcro wallet. That card was my passport to a deeper life, and I began spending countless afternoons at the library, surrounded by towers of books and literacy posters featuring pop culture icons of the eighties and nineties such as David Bowie and Shaquille O'Neal.

Reading is fundamental, some of the posters said, a sentiment that remains relevant today. In the midst of political turbulence and a barrage of attacks on the media, the arts, an education, it would do us all well to return to our libraries and reflect on that statement, to immerse ourselves in the written word, and in literature in particular.

Countless studies have shown the value of reading and what it can offer the mind and soul of the person willing to slip into another world for a few hours. Reading provides escape, a means of trading one's reality for another, which can be a balm. Reading offers information, facts and truths about history, politics, religion, and peoples around the world. But perhaps more importantly, reading contributes to building a deep reservoir of empathy within a person, a characteristic that is vital to being a citizen. By offering both escape and information, reading allows us to ponder the perspectives of characters or places different from our own, and to consider how those points of view might compare and relate to our own personal experiences. It tears down walls instead of building them.

There are many voices and experiences with which to empathize in this issue of *Appalachian Heritage.* There's the woman on a quest for love and understanding on the manicured streets of Dollywood in Leah Hampton's moving short story "Sparkle," and the couple negotiating the demands of purchasing a home and enduring a hard winter in Michael Croley's "Last Light." Courtney Balestier sings of West Virginia's signature food in her essay "The Poetry of Pepperoni Rolls," while Bill King contributes a lyrical elegy to the outdoors in "Trout Flashes." In her poems, Kentucky Poet Laureate George Ella Lyon takes us across the pond to the banks of the River Ouse, where the great Virginia Woolf ended her life, and to the Outer Hebrides, where time and memory are fluid and circular. Warner James Wood offers a haunting cycle of poems centered on rural life—a small town where women have their nails done at a salon called Alimony, where "the dog at the gate was a warning." We are also proud to announce the winners of the 2016 Denny C. Plattner Awards, given to the finest pieces of fiction, creative nonfiction, and poetry published in the magazine last year—work that moves, transports, and transforms.

Now, more than ever, we need our literature to do just that. ■

2016 DENNY C. PLATTNER AWARDS

The annual Plattner Awards were established in 1995 by Kenneth and Elissa Plattner to honor their late son and his love of writing. The awards are given to the finest pieces of fiction, creative nonfiction, and poetry that appeared in *Appalachian Heritage* during the previous year. Winners receive a $200 prize, and both winners and honorable mentions are awarded a handsome cherry wooden book rack designed and manufactured by Berea College Crafts.

FICTION

Judged by Amanda Jo Runyon, editor of The Pikeville Review

Winner: Chelyen Davis, "Junebug"
Honorable Mention: Elaine Fowler Palencia, "Dark Stars"

CREATIVE NONFICTION

Judged by Karen Salyer McElmurray, author of Surrendered Child: A Birth Mother's Journey

Winner: Amelia Fowler "Geographies of Pluto"
Honorable Mention: Tessa McCoy, "A Queen in My Blue Jeans"

POETRY

Judged by Anne Shelby, author of Appalachian Studies *and* The Adventures of Molly Whoopie

Winner: Rebecca Gayle Howell, "Audre Lorde was a Secret Hillbilly: A liturgy for the 21st Century"
Honorable Mention: Ron Houchin, "Gospel River"

SPARKLE

LEAH HAMPTON

Inside the candyfloss pink ticket booth, Mavis—that's what her name tag said—shifted her massive cardiganed breasts off the counter and looked out the customer window to see if there was anybody behind us.

"Now, it's not her usual thing," Mavis said when she'd decided we were alone. "But."

Behind me, James tensed. I figured it was going to be some kind of sales pitch for Splash Country, Dolly's water park nearby. James and I did not want to go to Splash Country. It was November, and it was raining. Mavis looked me square in the face.

"Bu-ut," Mavis dropped her twang to an emphysemal whisper, "*Dolly*... is in the park today." She twitched her mouth and pursed it to the side, satisfied with herself, then placed her hands primly on the candyfloss windowsill.

"No shit," I said.

"Oh, yes ma'am," said Mavis. Her hands went pat, pat, softly.

"James, did you hear that?" I looked at him and those eyebrows of his. James has these eyebrows that tell you everything. They raised up—a good sign.

"Well, that makes things interesting," he said.

Heat tingled up the outside of my neck and into my cheeks. I stared into the little booth. Mavis winked. "I think I just peed a little," I said. Mavis thought that was funny.

"You go down there to the right," Mavis said, "and they's a little thee-ater. Along about 2:30, she'll be in there."

My breath hitched. James closed in behind me until I could feel the warmth of him. Or maybe not the warmth. The ions of him? Electrons, crackling back and forth. That's how it is with certain people, now and then in life. You feel them even when they're not touching you.

"Is she"—my turn to whisper—"Oh, Miss Mavis, will she sing?"

Mavis's face looked like a sack of dough, but I wanted to kiss it. Since I was thirteen I have wanted to meet Dolly Parton, to exist for a minute in that cloud of glittery badassness. I don't even like country music. Just Dolly. All that *light*; she brings light into the world, or did into mine when I was a kid.

In junior high, I'd sneak-watch VHS tapes of her. I'd plug my daddy's big stereo earphones into the back of the TV set so he wouldn't hear me. I spent most of my time making sure Daddy didn't wake up from his naps on the sofa. He'd punch the shit out of anybody who didn't let him sleep all afternoon. I'd patch into those earphones and whisper-sing Nine-to-five, Nine-to-five for hours, squatted on the living room rug. I never told my friends or watched those tapes with anybody. Dolly's just about the only cheesy thing I can stand. I am not a cheesy person. Mavis was promising me something big here.

"No, honey," Mavis soothed. "It's an industry thing. A theme park conference? It's big wigs and such, park owners. Folks here from as far away as Knott's Berry Farm." She shifted back and rolled herself onto her little stool. I was glad the Dollywood people let Mavis have a stool in her ticket booth. She probably got tired standing all day. Mavis looked out the front window of her booth, the one facing into the park. "I

After he eased by, he turned and gave me a come-on-already-let's-go look. So I went.

don't reckon Dolly'll sing for those suited-up types. She's just gonna put in an appearance, do the welcome."

"Oh, I see," I said. My feet settled back into my shoes.

"But you never know. She knows people like for her to. And now," Mavis leaned forward, "there'll still be music. Some good musicians in the park today, on all the corners."

James started to shuffle past me. We already had our tickets. He put his hand right below my bra strap as he made his way past. The warmth spread out from where his hand was, all over my back. After he eased by, he turned and gave me a come-on-already-let's-go look. So I went.

"All right, well, thank you so much for telling us," I said to Mavis.

"Sure thing. 2:30, now. The orange doors." Mavis hopped off her stool and put her happy theme park face on for the next customer, even though there wasn't one. Most of the parking lots had been empty when we arrived. She called after us, "We're so glad to have you visiting with us here in Dollywood!"

I'm not obsessed with Dolly Parton or anything. I've only been to Dollywood four times in my whole life. I just wanted an excuse to be alone with James. He was only here for a few more days, and half of that was taken up with beer tours in Asheville and meetings in his old department. I couldn't get him alone at the house, either, because Pete kept muscling in. Also, Pete had been super touchy with me all week, all honey this and baby that, like all of a sudden we haven't been married for nine years. It made me itch.

We walked forward into the entrance gazebo. An elderly man with suspenders and an old timey mustache took our tickets.

"Nice 'stash," James mumbled, one eyebrow raised.

Then we swooped out of the gazebo and into the park. All the colors and music stopped James in his tracks. James had never been to Dollywood. I paused and let him get accustomed. It's a lot to take in if it's your first time.

"Come on, Dorothy," I said, "Get your slippers on!"

It was early November, so there were no Christmas decorations up yet. The wind greyed everything over, and the mountains slumped brown and spindly above us, with no leaves left anywhere. We probably picked just about the dullest, drabbest day to go to such a place. But it's like Dolly made the park so that it would be nice even in weather like that, because all that color she brings came right at us in a friendly way. The soft blue of the kiddie play area sat low at the edge of view, and the pastels from the Gospel Music House windows eased us onto the main path towards the roller coasters. Nothing garish or harsh about it.

James got moving soon after the initial shock of the place. We walked to the right until we got to the candy stores. A wide, bright path led towards the county fair rides. Beyond that were the steam train, the bird sanctuary, roller coasters, old timey shops, and on and on. From where we stood, the layers of the park loomed in blurry, then blurrier layers of neon and noise, one behind the other, getting indistinct and higher, just like the Blue Ridge does on a fine day.

"Whoa," James said, swaying towards a lavender storefront. "Do you smell that?"

I nodded. Be breezy, I thought. Don't spoil anything. This is the man you love.

Nobody knows I love James. Nobody. I can't breathe it out to anyone, because all our friends work at the college and know Pete. Besides, it's just about the most embarrassing thing in the world, to need a man you can't have, aren't married to. But I still thought *this is the man you love* to myself down deep.

That's why we came to Dollywood. That's why I picked a day that Pete had to teach, a day James wasn't giving any presentations, to suggest this trip. I pretended it was a whim that morning, something I'd just thought of. After Pete left for the lab, I sat at the breakfast table and laced this careful pattern of chatter with James to get him to come here with me. I know I just work in the bursar's office, but I'm pretty smart when I want to be.

One other thing I know is, even though he doesn't love me, James thinks I'm the funniest person in the world. He always says that, and he always talked to me when I came to department parties, and sometimes took me out to lunch, just the two of us.

When he first started teaching at the college, James picked Pete as his research partner for an NSF grant he got. All about efficient light refraction on metallic particles, which Pete knew about. Pete did his master's at the college, and then he got hired on at the lab right before we met. On our first dates, Pete would talk about his work in a slow, plodful way that made me feel safe. Here was a man with purpose, someone you didn't have to be scared of waking. Pete let me be clumsy without picking on me, took me to Georgia to his parents' house, which always smelled like pot pourri and clean money. I married him mostly because he asked.

James showed up a few years after, and he took to Pete right away. James says Pete missed his chance at a bona fide scientific career, that Pete knows more than anybody about what they do. But Pete isn't much for moving outward. He stayed plodful, stuck to the lab and his regularities. When I started to complain about the sameness in our life a few years back, Pete quit touching me. Or maybe I quit touching him. It doesn't matter now, after how long it's been.

Anyhow, James came, and a switch got thrown inside me. It didn't take any time at all before James decided he liked me as much as he dug Pete. Like I said, I can be smart, and I'm pretty enough to get a man to buy me lunch now and then. There were even times when I thought James might love me back, just a little, because of how he'd look at me when he thought I wasn't noticing. Then he took a job down in the Piedmont at a fancier school, and now every time I see him it's like starting over from scratch.

But for the four years he was here, we saw each other a lot—twice a week sometimes. We smoothed together so easy. James isn't from here, so he liked that I knew about the mountains. He'd ask me where to hike, which trees were blooming in the spring. He liked the stories I told about my family especially. His favorite was about the time my cousin Bigun climbed in the washer at our papaw's house when we were kids and got himself stuck.

We called him Bigun because he was a foot taller than anyone else we ever saw. I used to love playing with him because he treated me so gentle. Bigun used to tell me I was dainty. We'd play rock-paper-scissors, and Bigun always let me win, even though he was older than me and knew better. He'd wait for me to count three and flatten my fingers, then he'd make a meaty fist at the last second and smile out of every part of his face. It took both my hands spread out wide to paper over Bigun's rock.

James was eating a muffin at the hippie coffee shop by the campus library when I told him that yarn about Bigun getting stuck in the washer. He laughed so hard he choked on a muffin chunk. There were little muffin bits on my clothes when I

I got to pat James on the back and hold his shoulder and ask close if he was all right...

walked out and headed back to my desk, but I didn't mind. I got to pat James on the back and hold his shoulder and ask close if he was all right, even though I knew he was fine.

Three weeks before James came back for this visit, I found an old Dollywood souvenir mug at the Methodist thrift store. I bought it for a quarter. This morning after Pete left, I gave James that mug when he said he wanted more coffee. I asked him about his plans, even though I knew them. I'd looked up his schedule in the department secretary's office. I brought him his coffee and spun chatter for a few minutes. I kept him laughing, dazzled, then finally struck, *oh, hey.... you know what we should do?* and pointed at the mug, with Dolly's face on it and a big chip on her boob. Breezy.

I'd been wanting to bring him here ever since I found out he was coming for a whole week this time and staying at our house. Finding that mug was proof, a sign. I wanted to go to the brightest place I could think of and stare at James for as long as I could before he was gone again.

James is normal handsome, nothing special. He's kind of bald, and he has this goofy left eye that doesn't sit on his face the same way as his other one. But I love him; have since the first day I saw him. For all my sins, I love a hairless, lop-eyed chemist so bad it makes my whole body hurt when I so much as sit next to him. It hurts way inside, like cramps or sickness.

It hasn't been a problem lately, because James hasn't been here. He still visits for this one silver project he still works on, but that's twice a year at most. I think about him though, just as much as I did for the four years he was here. I keep waiting for that storm of feeling to go away or settle in me somewhere far down, but it hasn't. I figure it won't ever. Once I get an idea I tend to hang onto it pretty tight.

Maybe I am a cheesy person after all. I don't know. But James said yes when I offered to bring him to Dollywood, and he laughed when he said it, and that he couldn't think of a better way to spend his free day, that he'd be ready by ten, and we could go. So it worked, my spinning and scheming. That's all I cared about.

"Caramel," James said. His eyes were closed, his body facing the candy storefront. "We could get caramel apples. Do they have those?"

"We haven't even seen anything yet," I said. I pulled him down the path. I tried to sound chummy, so I had an excuse to lean into him. I couldn't smell any caramel. I could only smell the cedarwood tang of the soap he uses. I made sure I bought some before he came and put it in the spare bathroom. "Don't go soft on me so soon. There's hoot owls and roller coasters and all kinds up there. And we're going to Dolly's house--you have to see that. Candy's for later."

The sky looked like dirty quilt batting, and we walked past the sausage and pepper stand, the bluegrass gazebo, and a bunch of other stuff, waiting for a drop of sunlight. Mavis was right; some of the music was pretty good.

We got to the center of the park, and I showed James to Dolly's house, the one she grew up in. It's right where Dolly wants it, beside a bunch of lit-up signs for attractions and souvenir shops, with about five different places to eat circled around it. The cabin is on an island in the middle of all that bustle, just below the railroad bridge at the main intersection, so nobody forgets where Dolly came from.

James stepped up on the walkway with just his toe tips and read the sign carefully while I stood behind him. Then he said, "Are we allowed in?" He turned to me, and his face was like a boy's. I don't imagine very many people ever get to see his face like that.

I nodded and pointed to the sign, and we went inside. The tour only takes a minute, because Dolly grew up in a three-room house. They put most of the historical stuff, like her gowns and her coat of many colors, in her personal museum further down in the park. That museum's called Chasing Rainbows. Here in the cabin, glass barriers keep everyone out to preserve the place exactly as it was when she was a little girl. A sack of flour still sits by the stove, and the wallpaper is nothing but old newspapers.

All the noise of the park, the rides, the railroad, all of it drains away inside Dolly's cabin. The only thing we could hear was the boats swirling through the Smoky Mountain River Rampage down the hill. Each boat goes around a track and gets to a point where the fake rocks squirt river water all over the passengers. The whole thing works on a timer, I guess, because James and I walked along so softly inside that old place, and he whispered all his comments and questions to me, and everything hushed into respectful silence, except for about every twenty seconds or so, when we'd hear *thock-thock-shwhoosh.*

We finished the cabin tour and came out by the railroad bridge, and James said, "Well, that was incongruently tasteful." He knitted up his forehead and walked up towards the blacksmith shops. "She's really something, isn't she? Quite a beginning." He turned back to the cabin and regarded it from a higher vantage point.

Then he peered at me. His face wasn't boyish now; he looked detached, like he was researching something. He lifted his head and jutted his chin back down the hill towards Dolly's cabin. "Did you grow up in a place like that?"

Well, I mean please. My face went hot, and my stomach whomped fiercely. I couldn't decide if I was heartbroken or pissed. I tried to slow my breathing so my gut wouldn't hurt.

"No, Professor," I said. I crossed my arms and looked up the hill, away from him, towards the sunlight diffused behind all that dirty cotton batting. I was looking for the blue wings of the eagle coaster way up top. "I had plumbing and everything."

"Oh. Oh, right. I'm sorry, Beth."

"Heck, I even read a few books when I was a kid, when I wasn't losing teeth." I turned back to him and raised my chin. "Even managed to gra-jee-ate college."

"Of course. I didn't mean it like that."

"You want lunch?" I started walking. "Let's get some peppers and sausage."

"Beth, I'm sorry."

"Sure, fine. Just... you know. I'm not a country-fried fool or anything."

"I know that. I know it."

The whitewater boats *thock-shwooshed* again, far down the hill.

"It's just that I think you're like her," James said. He sounded far away. "Like Dolly."

"Quit looking at my tits, doc."

"No, really." I knew he was trying to smile, but I wouldn't look at him. I followed a crack in the black top under my foot. It went on forever.

"I intended it as a compliment," he said. "Of course, you dress much more simply." He seized on a word and blurted, "More refined."

Then he rubbed his head, put his hands in his pockets, and shrugged roughly. He rocked on his feet and leaned against the sign for Aunt Granny's Kitchen. I remembered then that not everyone thinks James is as beautiful as I do. Scientists move like awkward birds, and he does have that thing with his left eyeball, after all. So I let go of the insult. At least he'd tried to make up for it by calling me refined.

"How long til 2:30?" I asked.

James bent deeply to pull his hand from his pocket and frowned at his watch. His forehead scrunched up into a maze of wrinkles. "We've got about an hour." He turned and squinted at the eagle coaster on the hill.

For the record, the eagle coaster at Dollywood kicks ass. It looks like a giant bird, and the seats don't have a floor. People swing their legs free and scream their faces off on that thing. I've never ridden on it, because every time I've been to Dollywood that coaster is shut down for bees. Apparently there are bee colonies up on top of the hill, and Dolly doesn't want to mess with them or move them. So instead, if the bees are lively in summertime, they put up a special sign with honey pots and smiling bumblebees on it, and no one can ride the eagle coaster until they settle down into their hives.

It was late autumn now, with all the sun and leaves over, so no bees. The eagle was running—a giant raptor swaying above us, all blue and shiny, even under the dark, low clouds.

James watched the blue wings of the coaster for a second and said, "I don't really do stuff like that anymore. It twinges my back."

I watched a few little kids run screaming up the hill towards the bird and clenched my jaw. My mother never used to bother telling me to have babies, because she knows I don't want any. Kids are supposed to make you tender, but I never feel any closeness inside me when I see one. Anytime I see children, they seem far away.

But lately when she visits Mama says it—get pregnant already. Then she shakes her head at me and says I'm gloomy.

We went to the orange doors just like Mavis said, and it turned out Mavis is kind of a blabbermouth, because there must have been two hundred people already in line.

She says our house is too quiet. It took her years to figure out Pete doesn't hit me, because she just figures that's what everybody lives with. She thinks the way I grew up is normal.

My mother. She sees I'm missing something, but she doesn't know what it is.

It took me a second to let go of the idea of finally riding the eagle coaster. I breathed out slow and said, "Well, you want lunch then?" I put a little sing-song in my voice to tease him, "Yo-u can have can-dy af-ter..."

He smiled, but only from one side of his face, then bowed and swooped his hand toward the food stalls like a butler in some old movie. "Sausage and peppers it is, madame."

We found a picnic area with seats made out of old barrels sawed in half and smushed butt side up into the concrete. James didn't talk much over lunch, so I told him another story about Bigun to entertain him. This story was more recent, after Bigun grew up, a year or so before I met James. I told about Bigun getting drunk and shooting his rifle into the Dairy Queen sign when they forgot to put the peanuts on his sundae. I didn't tell James about Bigun crashing his pickup a few days after that, or how he lingered in the ICU, broken and swollen like an angry tick, for six weeks before he finally passed. I didn't say how I spread out my textbooks on the plastic sofa outside his room and studied for all my semester exams, peeking in every now and then to see if Bigun's fingers would twitch hello for me. I didn't want to talk about sad things before we saw Dolly. Bigun's real name was Charles, so I told him that instead.

A little after two we wound our way to the theater. We went to the orange doors just like Mavis said, and it turned out Mavis is kind of a blabbermouth, because there must have been two hundred people already in line. A lot of them were suited-up types, with name tags from a bunch of different theme parks pinned to their lapels. But about half the crowd was regular people like us. I wondered where they'd all been hiding up to now; the park had been empty all afternoon.

"Betrayed," James said, shaking his head. "I assumed our ticket lady was keeping this between friends."

"It'll be fine. We'll get a seat," I replied. "Doesn't matter as long as we get to see her."

James nodded and we got in line. We filed in through the big orange doors, and we found seats way at the back of the main floor, off to the far left. The seats were dark blue and thick cushioned. Everything on the stage was blue, too. Blue curtains, and a big TV screen with nothing on it except the royal emptiness you get on channels you haven't paid for. James said he figured we'd have to sit through some conference talk before we got to see Dolly, and he asked if I was up for that. I said yes, I'd sat through my share of boring presentations with Pete. Turned out we didn't have to wait long at all.

A round, standard-issue Yankee in a navy suit came up on stage to give a speech about the national federation of theme park executives, or whatever it was called, and how pleased they were to be there, and what the schedule for today's keynote event would be. He was just getting to the part where he asked everyone to check their conference schedule booklet when a gleeful surge rumbled over from the right side of the house. I looked across the stage, and there she was.

Dolly Parton, right there in front of me.

They say celebrities look smaller in person, and it's a disappointment because you expect them to be taller or more imposing. When Dolly walked out, my mouth dropped open and I shot out of my seat. As I watched her, I thought two things at the same time: that she was the littlest, tiniest thing I'd ever seen, and that she wasn't a disappointment at all. All the typical stuff you think of when you think of Dolly Parton—shine and light and makeup and hair and boobs—all of it was perfect. She looked so totally and exactly like I wanted her to, I almost didn't believe it was her. Her being so little made me think she was a doll, a fancy toy for rich kids. Then I forgot about her smallness and held my hands together tight and watched her walk towards the guy in the suit. He had dropped his conference booklet and was beaming silently.

I don't care who you are. Everybody in that room was overcome. James shot to his feet right along with me, and he was clapping and watching her, then turning to me and laughing, back and forth. Dolly looked so beautiful, and she was smiling and waving to everyone. She stood there for just the right, dignified amount of time, not too long, and let the crowd applaud her. A sound guy in a black t-shirt ran out and handed her a microphone.

"Well, hey, everybody!" Dolly Parton giggled at us. We all waved and applauded some more, and she waved back. James crossed his arms and put one elbow on his hand so he could raise the opposite hand to his chin and rest it there. Every last one of us, even the suits who were acting businesslike while we were in line, all of us were transfixed.

Dolly must have known they'd have all blue up there, because she had chosen a gold outfit that stood out against the blue backdrop and popped off the stage. She had on a slinky gold satin dress, sleeveless. It glistened softly down to her knees. That dress would have been a classy number by itself, but it's Dolly, so over that dress she wore a jacket that I won't ever forget. The jacket looked like the finest lace, only it was bright gold and twinkly everywhere. It had to have been handmade, and it didn't look cheap. She stood in front of the big blue TV screen, and between that and the spotlight hitting her, the gold jacket reflected and refracted back and forth to build a fine, warm halo around her. I know that sounds crazy, and I'm not going to say she looked like an angel on top of a Christmas tree, but I'll bet that's what a bunch of us were thinking. James studies light-refracting particles, so he probably knew exactly what was making Dolly shine like that.

She didn't stay for long. Mavis was right; she had only come to welcome the conference attendees. Apparently that conference is a big deal in theme park circles. Dolly said she had come out today to tell all the theme park executives how glad she was that they had chosen Dollywood to host their big meeting. She talked about the history of the park, how it used to be called Silver Dollar City before she bought it and fixed it up.

Some woman behind me drawled, "That's right, you remember that, Dale? She saved the place. I used to come here and ride that ol' run down silver mine coaster." I nudged James to see if he'd heard.

Then Dolly made one of her usual jokes about her boobs, and she told the suits to be sure and tell her what they thought of her little ol' theme park, because she and her staff had worked hard to make it a great place for folks to come with their families. Then she thanked us again, and thanked the boring guy in the navy suit for letting her steal some of his time. She handed him the microphone and walked off waving and blowing kisses.

The audience clapped and hollered, but Dolly didn't come back out to sing. We settled down slowly, but the whole theater tingled for a long time after. Whatever electrons James shoots into me when he's nearby, Dolly's got a billion more of them, because everyone in there felt warm and happy. Mr. Blue Suit never stopped beaming while he said three times that Dolly was "marvelous." Then he said his colleagues should wait a minute for park visitors to file out of the theater, and then the conference would proceed on schedule.

We were all in such a good mood that nobody minded bustling and squishing past each other in the narrow aisles. As I shimmied towards the orange exit, I checked everyone's faces. All the suits looked tickled and loose. James and I said excuse me and I'm sorry a hundred times, and we got patted on the shoulder if we accidentally stepped on a foot or a briefcase. Dolly eases people.

When we got outside, I could tell that James was impressed. I asked him, "Well, was that the highlight of your week?" He put his hands on his hips and smiled with all his teeth, then he shrugged big. He didn't have to say anything. My whole body shook, but I kept my own thoughts inside so I wouldn't spoil his.

"You want to get that caramel apple now?" I asked. "The shop's over there."

James put one hand on his belly, and I noticed his fleece jacket was the same color as our theater seats. His face darkened. "I probably shouldn't. I just ate that sausage. Besides," he said, "who needs candy when you've got Dolly Parton?"

I laughed. "Nothing sweeter, right?"

"Yes, she really does have something. I was impressed. Dazzled, even." James patted his stomach, then arced his hand to indicate the park, the rides, Dolly, the wide, bright paths, Mavis in the ticket booth, everything. "All that glitters," he murmured.

We strolled through the candy shops but didn't buy anything. James took one look at the caramel apples and said they were as big as a baby's head. I pretended to look at cookbooks. Mostly I peeped at James between the bookshelves, especially when he walked through the lollipop section. Some of those lollipops span a foot across, and they stack up in rows along the walls. Against the swirling candy behind him, the subtlety of his dark blue jacket and his brown hair popped. He stood out the same way golden Dolly had popped on that blue stage, but it was like James was doing it in reverse, a negative of an old color photograph.

There's not much left to Dollywood once you get past the candy stores. We'd left all the rides and kids' stuff behind us. James wasn't interested in any of that. It was pretty much just the gift shop left. You can't leave Dollywood unless you go through that gift shop; it's the only exit.

I figured James would buy something since he hadn't ridden any of the rides. A little part of me hoped he'd buy *me* something, to thank me for bringing him, signify the day, so I remarked on a few items. I made sure not to be girly about it, but he didn't pick up or touch anything. I even found a mug exactly like the chipped one I bought at the Methodist thrift store. I showed him that. He nodded and *mm-hmmed* in a friendly way that meant no.

"You don't want a souvenir?" I finally asked. "It's the same as my mug from this morning, but without the crack on her tit."

James tilted his head. "I've got a bunch of luggage I need to take home."

"So, but, you had fun, right? Isn't this place a kick?"

"Yes, I'll admit I did have fun, actually." He chuckled again and turned away slightly. Then he mumbled, "To be honest, I was expecting Araby."

I rolled my eyes. What a thing to say. James squinted and leaned towards me.

"Araby," he said again slowly. "That's, uh... It's a story."

"Yeah." I plonked the Dolly mug back on the table and glared at a row of shot glasses to my right. "There's a copy of *Dubliners* on the shelf in the spare room. You can re-read it later."

"Oh, right. Sure. Sorry, I just assumed you wouldn't..."

"We should head back," I said. "It'll take us at least an hour and a half. More if it starts to rain."

I wondered whether he even noticed the mountains glowing lavender at their edges in the late afternoon gloom.

Those shot glasses. They all looked so clear and clean. The fluorescent bulbs above us shone straight down to the bottom of each one and made a pool of light that splashed up through their silver lettering.

"Yes, you're right," said James. "Hey, did you want to get anything for yourself? Those hats are sort of neat." He pointed to a high shelf lined with baseball caps covered in glittery butterflies. Butterflies are the symbol of Dollywood.

“I don’t wear hats.” I leaned into my hip. “We can catch a trolley back to the car.”

As I moved to go, I felt my fingers reach out to the shot glasses. I grabbed one and stuffed it in my pocket in one blunt, smooth swipe. There.

We walked past the stuffed animals and toys to the door, back out into the cold late afternoon. To the right, a series of ropes wound along a plain concrete tunnel. The end of each rope marked where visitors could wait for a lift. We moseyed along the tunnel, me with my hands shoved in the back pockets of my jeans, shoulders wide, James hunched over thinking to himself about something that was probably far away from here. I wondered whether he even noticed the mountains glowing lavender at their edges in the late afternoon gloom.

When we got to the front of the line, he said, “Well, I guess we can die happy, now that we’ve seen Dolly Parton in all her glory.”

I snorted. “Hardly.” I don’t know if it was his question about living in a shack, or not getting to ride the eagle coaster, or skipping the gift shop, or what, but all of a sudden I felt hard towards James. He didn’t know. It wasn’t his fault, but I hated him then, and I wanted the trolley to come soon, fast. Because I have all this love. I feel it in me and around me like those electric sparks that come out of magicians’ hands in old movies. The sparks crackle and swell all the time, but he doesn’t see it spilling out of me. I don’t understand that. Not at all.

“Oh?” James smiled back. He didn’t know. “So, what then, Miss Tennessee? What do you need to die happy?”

I sighed. I could see the trolley coming, a chain of long white golf carts strung together. They were hitched up loose, so the whole thing writhed like a huge maggot as it drove up. It turned from the entrance, from the ticket booths where we met Mavis, and came toward us.

"Take me to a hotel tonight," I said. I blinked hard. His face tilted; his eyebrows in three different positions each. I crossed my arms and stepped out to meet the trolley. It beeped and tooted all kinds of happy noises that echoed off the concrete and hurt my ears. "You do that," I said, "You take me away for a night, just once, and I'll go to my grave."

I could feel the rattle in my voice coming, the quiver that rises when you're about to cry, so I bit down and focused on the maggot stopping in front of us. A sharp laugh shot out of me. "But that's not going to happen, right? You're not going to fuck some redneck. So." I shrugged. "I guess I can't die."

I spat the last few words and climbed into an empty trolley seat.

"Goooood evening, folks!" the trolley driver chirped into the PA system. "We'll be on our way just as soon as everyone gets on safely."

Almost no one was waiting with us, but the trolley idled for a few minutes in case more people came looking for a ride. I don't know how long it took before James finally sat down next to me. I don't know if he stared at me, or laughed, or looked back at the eagle coaster and felt bad inside. I kept my eyes on the white floor of the maggot and waited to get hurt.

I sensed his electron warmth before too long. He scooted up close. The glinty shot glass had worked its way into the crevice between my hip and crotch. It sat there like a thick bullet.

"Elizabeth."

"Just fuck off for a minute, James."

"Awwwwwrighty folks," the trolley driver chirped again. "We are taking off, and we'll have you to your ve-hickles in no time. Please make sure your packages are secure, and hold on to your little ones."

"Is it..." James nodded at a perky trolley attendant who was waving frantic goodbyes to everyone on the maggot. "Have you always felt like this?"

"Yep."

We drove to Lot A and stopped. We were parked in Lot C.

"I'm shocked," he finally said. His eyes widened and he turned towards me. "I mean, I'm flattered, but I'm just—shocked." He touched his chest.

"How?"

"What?"

"How is that possible? How can you be shocked?"

"Well, I... Beth, you're married."

Pete. Fucking Pete. As if that counts as being married. Pete was an obstacle. He blocked everything. Pete could block the sun.

"You seriously don't notice it? This?" I pointed back and forth between us until James' eyes softened. "You never think about it."

"Yes, sure. I've thought about it. Of course I have."

Lot B, folks. This is Lot B.

"So what then? You don't think it would work? You don't even want a fling or anything? Jesus, why not get a little action when you're in town, at least?" I was keeping it breezy, even now.

James stared straight ahead for a full minute, until I figured he hadn't heard or he'd never answer me. The trolley was approaching our lot when he spoke again.

"If we were both single, if I still lived here, sure, maybe. But Beth. That's not the way things are. And Pete... you know," he shook his head and grunted with a harsh edge I'd never heard before. The maggot came to a stop. "Pete's a pretty good friend of mine."

"So okay then, folks!" the driver shouted. "This is Lot C. Please step out on the right, and thank y'all for visiting us here in Dollywood! We hope you had a great time today. Come see us again." The trolley radio squawked and fired up again. "Passengers going into the park, please step in on the left. Please secure your belongings and hang onto your little ones."

There were no passengers going into the park, no little ones. James and I stepped out on the right, I think. I wasn't paying attention, and I couldn't see in front me. My eyes were welled up and everything looked like frosted bathroom glass. I didn't cry, though.

It didn't take long to walk to the car. The lot was empty now. I held out my car keys to James and tried to keep my voice light. "You want to drive me home?"

He reached, curled his hand over the keys, and kept his arm held out to me for a long second. I looked at his fingers. They looked like mine, but stronger, more manly. I wanted to bend down and rest my cheek on them, soft like a newborn, for as long as I could, long enough to memorize his knuckles, the grooves at the base of his palm, how they felt against my skin. But I knew how girlish and strange that would seem, me bent double over somebody's fist in a cold, empty parking lot, and for no reason. It wouldn't mean anything to do it.

So instead I said, "We could take the back route, through the national park, instead of the interstate. It's just as quick."

It wasn't just as quick, but I didn't want to deal with all the traffic and neon signs in Gatlinburg or go too fast. The sky had been woolen all afternoon, and soon the daylight would be gone.

"Sure, Beth," he said, more breath than words. And I figured that was nice of him. He would take the wheel and leave me be all the way home.

As we pulled out, I thought about Dolly's gold jacket, how it floated on her like lacy sparkle wings, all the way down, almost to the floor. I couldn't fit one arm into a jacket like that without ripping it. Then I thought about the silver particles floating in tubes in the lab James and Pete used to share, the glitter soup they'd make for their experiments. I liked it when they made that stuff, but I was never allowed to get too close, because Pete said the particles were growing and forming, swapping and stealing atoms from each other, and even a fingerprint on the beaker could upset the balance.

All the delicate things in the world that shine like that. I looked back towards Dollywood, and I thought about all of them. They shine on their own, and they break if I ever try to get them in my hands. ■

ALIMONY

Across the street from Divine Intervention
Auto Repair, behind the Dairy Queen,
my mother opened a nail salon named Alimony.
The women inside are never my mother's age.
They are women born at home, who talk
of their dead husbands as if they wished they'd
killed them themselves. The boys nowadays,
they tell my mother, aren't like their fathers.
We know, they say, we raised them.
The women recall their firsts, their lasts,
explain the lost importance of setting the mood,
which, they say, is different than setting the table.
When asked a color, they all want rouge or mauve,
and they want a gloss. When my mother finishes,
she moves behind the women to see over their shoulders
as they raise their ringed fingers to eye level. They remain
there, the women and my mother, inspecting the smoothed
fresh paint, glancing at the mirror to see the palm reflected back.

WARNER JAMES WOOD

AND I REMEMBER IT NOW

I'd run the woods in furs stolen
from my mother's locked closet,
hoping for hunters in tree stands—
spend days crouched, unnoticed,
where lumberjacks felled pines.
I had exhausted all my options.
The beam didn't hold like it did
last time, and it had been so long
since that night my mother came
to my bedside, sank to her knees,
hands on the mattress, elbows out,
like a child at the edge of a pool.
I can hardly remember my mother
in three dimensions—in my head
she's a cardboard cutout on a rope.
But I can still see her thin fingers
pressed to her mouth, intercepting
the hot whispered breaths, directing
them up through opal colored nails.

WARNER JAMES WOOD

FIRST SATURDAY OF SPRING

The dog at the gate was a warning:
What was ours, was ours.
She was tied there when
the gate alone was not enough,
the wooden fence disassembled,
the hemlocks laid bare across the path removed.
What we had was not a lot:
A few acres lining a river bed,
forty-four wild turkey in the evenings
in winter. Each year, this day,
shots fire from guns not ours.
The birds do not stay after this.
It takes a year before their offspring
return. My father in his age
takes solace in our evening drives,
in counting the gang, watching it
faction in the weeks before hunting season,
when each male nests its hens for birth.
He mixed gunpowder in the dog's bowl, so she could be
fierce to intruders, could bite at headlights
and ground herself in the path. My father did not worry
about the dog, but when he found her
shot through the shoulder, left to bloat in the sun,
he knew that it was a warning, too. But not of what.

WARNER JAMES WOOD

MOON SONG

Tobacco dry, money
and a carnival on the way
again, the moon begins
her due-west march down
the aisle, donning thin clouds
as a veil. We take to our roofs,
guests at a wedding, and watch
as she shells out spotlight only
on us, our streets and tilled farm-
lands, until flashbulbs ignite
from our tin-topped gables
and we capture a light no one can
remember ever being so simple,
and that no one has reason
to believe will ever be this way
again. Kids hold out their tongues,
husbands hold hands with wives,
and I hold my breath, as though
passing through a tunnel where
the moon is at the end.

WARNER JAMES WOOD

TROUT FLASHES

BILL KING

1.

In the Blue Ridge mountains of southwestern Virginia, sitting on a rock that juts like a peninsula into a little stream called Back Creek, my twelve-year-old brother—wiry, already chiseled and lean—wets a piece of bread between the tip of his tongue and his front teeth, takes it out, balls it between his thumb and index finger, and then sticks it on a hook. He throws it into the current at the top of the hole and lets it drift down and down. Maybe you'll catch a trout, I say. *Ain't no trout in here,* he says, pulling up another mad-tail-flipping sucker, a fat-headed thing with horny bumps on its crown. I want to fish, too, but there is never room for both of us.

2. An Irish tale tells of the forlorn young lover of a murdered prince, who, in drowning herself in a pristine mountain lake, transforms into a white trout. She is caught by an evil soldier, who cuts the white trout's side, releasing her bleeding human form. She bids the terrified soldier to throw her back in the little lake so that she can await her lover's return, which he does in great haste, bloodying the water and giving us the beautiful pink-streaked rainbow trout. In South Carolina, my uncle once told me to rub dirt, mud, and leaves on my hand to hide my human scent. *Trout know,* he said. *They are the oldest and wisest fish you will ever catch.*

3. There are rainbow trout, lake trout, cutthroat trout, brown trout, and tiger trout. The only trout native to West Virginia, though, is the brook trout. They live throughout Appalachia but only in the coldest and purist mountain streams. They sport a beautiful vermicular pattern— from dark green back, to bluish sides, to pink to scarlet belly—and interspersed throughout this swirling sky of color is a galaxy of yellow and red spots like stars behind a day-blind sky. No photograph can capture a brook trout's beauty. That's why, each spring—with pungent ramps greening the darkest hillsides and maple leaves still small and bright as babies' hands—I can't help but go for them. If I'm lucky, I'll get to cradle one in my palm—half in and half out of the water—before watching him slip beneath churning bubbles, which pour downstream like spilled pearls.

4. Brook trout drop over fallen logs and shelving rock, into a deep and roiling hole, before settling in the shadow of a submerged boulder. Where they decide to stay, unless a fisher comes along and puts one in her creel, as heart-struck as a boy with a new ball. Mike Trout, the youngest in major league baseball history to hit 100 homeruns and steal 100 bases, smashes white balls with red stitching over fences throughout North America. They drop over walls like trout over a weir: into parking lots, under parked cars. And no one knows about them—ball or trout—when they step into their car, when they back out of wherever they are and head for highways at least two ridges removed from nowhere.

5. My 50-year-old friend Gordon loves to fish, but he acts like a boy when he catches a trout. Once we went up McGee run, which tumbles through the spruce, rhododendron and laurel of Cheat Mountain, before meeting the Shaver's Fork. It's hard to get there and you have to walk up the middle of the stream to navigate the tight confines of the holler. He put a picture of a brilliantly speckled 6-inch brookie on Facebook for his friends in Georgia to see. His face was flushed and red. His green eyes like stars sunk in a depthless pool. They made fun of his measly catch. *You do not understand,* he replied.

6. In Cormac McCarthy's post-apocalyptic novel, *The Road,* a father and son push a wobble-wheeled grocery cart down a broken road. They wend out of the Appalachians, through the Georgia piedmont, to the Gulf of Mexico, surviving roving bands of cannibalistic marauders, murderous thieves, and starvation. For as far as they can see, the landscape looks like a mountaintop removal site—flat, greenless, rocky, and worried by dust-devils and the thump-and-rumble memory of detonation. Mountaintop removal is the process by which energy companies extract thin seams of coal, by blowing the

tops off mountains and dumping them in narrow valleys. In the past few decades, 2000 miles of streams in West Virginia have been buried. Says McCarthy, "Once there were brook trout in the streams in the mountains . . . On their backs were vermiculate patterns that were maps of the world in its becoming. Maps and mazes. Of a thing that could not be put back. Not be made right again."

7. The brook trout is small and bright, with a tale to tell that must be told. To tell it, you have to find the wildest places left, which, from high above, just look like dark creases in a sea of green. But they want you to—the brookies, I mean—because their survival depends on those that believe in mazes and mystery, in the origins of the universe, and the untold beauty that resides in the heart of all things. ■

WHEN

When I think of that beach
when I think of where the planes landed
when I was a Barra boy
when I think of the generation
before the planes
when I ran, a little girl with braids flying
down the strand from my Ma to my Da
when I remember *being* the Da
hoisting my boy to my shoulders
walking home in twilight
sky the color of doves
when I remember being the Ma
stirring fish-head stew
in the iron pot over the fire
when I remember changing the straw
in our pallets, dreaming of a feather tick

I can see blisters on my least one's arm
when she bumped my hand
as I ladeled up dinner
I see her feet
in the straw shoes my ma plaited

and I am young again
wild as a girl
feisty as a boy
a man tall in his strength
a woman full in her giving

and the light of this earth
shines through me
and time is the way
we join hands

GEORGE ELLA LYON

MARCH 28, 1941

What they remember
is your drowning

not your Olympic swimming
not those dives
those ecstatic surfacings

not how you caught
what flashed
beneath the billows

not how you wrote
on the waves.

GEORGE ELLA LYON

SPRING

In memory of Martha

One winter in the late afternoon
my aunt and I took a drive
out into the countryside
and watched as the sun began to set
over icy fallow farm fields
its shallow oblique light
the very thing she wanted me to see
because it was beautiful.
Aunts you see run in my family
even though I only had one
she came from a long line
of strong aunts
mountain women
who fended for themselves
even taking in other people's children
like she took me in once
when as a young man
I thought I was going to die of AIDS
and the city had become a mortuary
so I had to get out.
One evening in early April
we stood outside listening
to chirping sounds
to peepers my aunt said
I didn't know what those were
baby frogs she told me.

JAY KIDD

LAST LIGHT

MICHAEL CROLEY

The house had the appearance of a French villa but it was here in the middle of Ohio. Icicles hung from its eaves and the beige brick was bright against the snow, which had melted and then frozen again, forming a crust that Edward's boots sank into once he stepped from the car.

"This might have been a mistake," he said.

Angela was at the front door, peering inside. "What do you mean?" she said over her shoulder.

"I don't think we're going to be able to get out of this driveway," he said, stomping his feet onto the porch.

"This one looks nice," she said, turning back to the small windows beside the door.

The wind pressed against them and tangled Angela's hair. Edward studied the driveway, assessing its grade, the bald tires of their SUV, which he had been too cheap to buy with four-wheel drive.

"Where's Melissa?" He put his hands in his pockets and braced himself against the cold. "Did you text her?"

"She's on her way."

In truth he didn't want to be here. He had reluctantly agreed to resume the house hunt after a three-month hiatus because they had run into Melissa at the grocery and she told them she had the perfect home.

Melissa's headlights flashed and her German SUV, with all four of its powered tires, dug into the snow-covered drive with a satisfying crunch. The house sat on a knob that overlooked a flat parcel of land that stretched to a passel of trees. The sun was just at their tops, falling below the horizon and turning the clouds a magnificent peach.

"Sorry I'm late," Melissa said. She held the MLS sheets out to Angela and punched in the code on the lockbox.

Angela turtled her head to keep her ears out of the wind. The sun broke through a bank of windows opposite the entryway and the wheat colored floors seemed to flare once Melissa managed to open the door, and they were inside, standing in sheets of light.

"That's impressive," Angela said, turning to Edward. He only nodded. They had a rhythm and routine in these things.

They didn't say much and didn't tour the house together. Both of them often left Melissa alone in the kitchen as they each separately went through basements and bedrooms, tugged at windowsills, and flipped on lights.

Home buying was such strange business, Edward thought. He often tried to recreate life inside the blank space, thinking of the lives that been lived in these rooms, the meals taken at the kitchen counter, the arguments shouted past the walls.

"What do you think?" Angela said, coming toward him.

"Seems like a lot of space." He stood by a pair of patio doors, watching the ebbing light as the sun sunk beneath the trees. "Maybe too much."

"I don't think so," she said. "I like this patio."

The field below the house was also crusted with ice and the trees' shadows were merging with evening.

The brick pavers were arranged in a herringbone pattern. They were neat and level. Edward had only looked at a few rooms: the master bedroom and what would be their child's room if they decided to try again. The field below the house was also crusted with ice and the trees' shadows were merging with evening.

"It's a lot of money," he said.

"We can afford it."

"Barely."

"That's not true. We've been saving."

"I'd like to save more. Wait a year."

He saw her suppress a sigh and then flash her eyes to Melissa, who was punching away at her phone in the kitchen, oblivious of them. She was not a good realtor. "Not this again," Angela said. "Just once I wish you didn't do this to me. We've been looking so long. You're never sure about anything."

He could not summon any conviction to argue this point. He was serially unsure about nearly everything, always allowing his mind to race to dozens of worst-case scenarios. He wanted to feel the solidity of their marriage, to forget about the miscarriage and the corners of their rented house it had driven them to. He still loved her and he could tell, in certain but rare light-hearted moments, she him, but she was more broken than he.

"Should we talk to her about the house?" Angela said, nodding toward the realtor.

"Yes," he said.

Melissa ran them through the pros and cons, the neighborhood, and how the market might increase its inventory when spring finally arrived. Edward was skeptical about a future within the house, but he let Angela ask her questions about plumbing, HVAC, roofs, the schools and the neighborhood. By the time they walked back outside, night had come on and he no longer saw the trees. Melissa pulled away, tires spinning at first, then the tread took hold and she was off.

"Well?" Angela said, waiting, it had seemed, to make sure the woman was out of earshot.

"I think we're stuck." Edward kicked behind a tire.

"Not about the car," she said.

"I want to buy it," he said.

Her eyes brightened. "You do?"

He didn't but he thought if he could give her this piece of happiness, swallow his own fears, then they might find their way back to each other and how it had been coming home from the doctor's office after that first ultrasound and the good dreams they had not known until the moment they heard the child's heartbeat.

"Yes," he said. "It'll be our home."

"I don't believe you," she said.

"Call Melissa and tell her to start the paperwork."

"Are you serious?" she said, a smile widening.

"I am," he said.

"Maybe we should think about this more. In the car. I'm cold."

The blower hummed warm air over their toes. "We've looked at so many houses, can this be the one?" she said.

His heart beat fast. "I think we found it," he said. His chest tightened, a flash of heat burned his sternum.

"And you really like it?"

If it will make you happy, I would buy you ten houses like this one, he whispered in his head.

"We're going to buy this house, aren't we?" she said, allowing herself to be happy.

"Let's go have supper and call Melissa," he said.

She put the car in gear but the tires only spun, rocking the vehicle into the ice.

He stepped outside, leaving his door open. "We're in pretty deep."

"Can you push us?" she said.

"I can try," he said.

The vehicle's warm exhaust turned white in the cold air. Through the back window, the curls of her hair were lit from the dashboard. He tapped the glass and motioned for her to roll her window down. Then he took a stance, his hands pressed flat against the lift gate, and told her to gun it. The engine revved loud and he pushed so hard blood rose to his head and the muscles in his chest constricted. His feet slipped but he caught himself and pushed harder, but they did not move. Breathless, he stood and went back to her window. His front was covered with mud. "I'm a mess," he said. They both shared a small laugh.

"We'll call a tow truck," she said. "Come get out of the weather and sit with me." She reached her hand out to him and he took it. A smile was in her eyes and he felt her fingers move across the back of his hand. He bent down and kissed her, felt how cold his own nose was pressed against hers. Then he stood and looked past her shoulder, imagining a thousand sunsets like the one from earlier, the way the evening had clung to every bit of the sun's last light. ■

UNLIKELY PAIRINGS

Building on the rubble of our lives,
we grope for solace in unlikely pairings

like a cinderblock cavern signed Ammo
& Marital Aids, or these boys dowsing

paint chips in Ace Hardware for their band's name—
Buckram Binding, Hubbard Squash—hoping

it might open doors in Nashville, miles
from meth labs infesting hollers, those porches

where they learned to pick and slide. I hitch
onto their hope, let it tow me down the years

to the swimming hole and the old tire I'd ride—
swinging away from the bank with a whoop,

then a plunge, my lithe body breaking
the ice-green water, never looking back.

GAIL TYSON

READING TOGETHER

Out the window, hoarfrost beards the mountain;
inside, Buck stove flames ripple, dog snores,
brandy flares in throat. Snug in twin armchairs,

we dwell in two worlds: your Vikings pillage,
slaughter; my plucky English detective
scours the village, building her case. Shared

solitude anchors us, as always
until I look across the room, study
the face I've loved for twenty years, turned

inward, lured to a faraway place
beyond my reach, and foreboding chills,
wills the woman on my page to stow away

on your longship, under the dragon-head bow,
determined to solve this mystery:
how in an instant six feet between us

gapes, silence flat and sharp as a blade.

GAIL TYSON

AN *APPALACHIAN HERITAGE* INTERVIEW WITH

JULIE HENSLEY

"Most artists carry their childhood landscape like a native language," poet and fiction writer Julie Hensley states, an observation that contains the framework for her captivating short story collection *Landfall,* recently published by The Ohio State University Press. Winner of the Non/Fiction Collection Prize, the book centers on Conrad's Fork, a small Kentucky town conjured so vividly that, in the words of bestselling novelist Amy Greene, "it's easy to forget [it] is a fictional place."

That's due in no small part to Hensley's childhood in Big Stone Gap, Virginia, where Elizabeth Taylor famously choked on a chicken bone and the spectre of John Fox, Jr. continues to haunt the hills. The stories and people she encountered there continue to inform her writing, she says, a legacy to which she pays tribute in this recent interview with *Appalachian Heritage.*

■ ■ ■

JASON HOWARD: *Landfall* is billed as "A Ring of Stories," and it does seem as if there is a circular structure—the unbroken circle as the Carter Family would call it—to the collection. Can you talk about that?

JULIE HENSLEY: I struggled for a long time with knowing the book was finished. Many of the stories were part of my MFA thesis at Arizona State University, and I regularly submitted many different versions of *Landfall* to first book contests for over a decade. I kept changing the sequencing, occasionally adding or omitting a story. The book was a perpetual runner-up in so many contests—the Flannery O'Connor Award, the Katharine Anne Porter Prize, the Linda S. Bruckheimer Award. Finally, it won the Everett Southwest Literature Award, a contest which includes a generous prize but does not actually publish the book. I told myself I would give the project one more year of revision and one more round of submission, then I would let it go and move on.

The following summer, when I was teaching for a month in Mexico, I wrote three mornings a week at Café Montenegro, a little coffeehouse off the central plaza in San Miguel de Allende. As I crafted what became "Expecting," I felt *Landfall* click into place as a book. It was like I'd been jiggling a key in a lock for years, and suddenly, as the voices of Cora and Grace emerged, the bolts gave and shifted. When that door opened, so many things settled into place—characters I subconsciously had been worrying about just reappeared, pushing their own stories to fruition in the periphery of the narrative. The book itself suddenly, literally came full circle.

I might have called *Landfall* "A Novel-in-Stories" or "A Cycle of Stories." Certainly, books I've heard ascribed with those labels (Louise Erdrich's *Love Medicine*, Anne Tyler's *Dinner at the Homesick Restaurant*, Alice McDermott's *After This*) were influential. But I gravitated toward the idea of a ring or circle because of the way that shape conveys both continuity and paralysis. A circle goes on for always, but it also creates a kind of enclosure, and by extension, a kind of exclusion. In my experience, small towns can do both: offer protection or cage one inside a tight pattern of conformity. The same might be said for family communities. You could argue certain stories in my book are as much "Ring of Fire" as "Will the Circle Be Unbroken." Ultimately, I believe the book is about connection, though. I want it to be hopeful.

JH: The book is mostly set in Conrad's Fork, a fictional small town in Kentucky, and you do a great job in this book of showing how the supposedly simple, ordinary lives of small town Americans are actually rich and complex and stressful. Did you feel a sort of responsibility to do that as a writer from a small town, or did that theme just emerge by instinct?

Julie Hensley

HENSLEY: I always feel a responsibility to my characters to make them real and to make their lives matter. Conrad's Fork is an amalgamation of some of the towns in Virginia where I was raised and some of the towns in Eastern Kentucky that make me feel nostalgic and homesick these days. When I began working on the stories, I really saw the Shenandoah Valley as the fictional landscape in my mind, specifically the town of Elkton. My family moved to a small farm there just as I began middle school. Long ago, when the town was just a trading post, it actually was called Conrad's Store. At first, the responsibility I felt to that geography and its people was almost overwhelming. I think I wanted to do everyone justice; I didn't want to mar what was so acutely familiar. But fiction is all about trouble, so, of course, that would never do. Once I let myself fully start to imagine the landscape, setting it in a fictional county in Kentucky, the writing became much freer, and ironically the characters grew more complex.

JH: You make use of the second person in a couple of the stories, and to me there's always an inherent risk with that choice—it can sound stilted or off-putting. But your use of it reads and feels so natural. How did you manage that?

HENSLEY: Thank you for that praise. Second person point of view is always tricky, but sometimes it works beautifully: Junot Diaz's "The Cheater's Guide to Love," Pam Houston's "How to Talk to a Hunter," and Lorrie Moore's "The Kid's Guide to Divorce" are great examples. That point of view, when it's working well, is really a gradation of first person point of view—the narrator isn't talking to the reader, but rather to herself. For me, certain characters insist on a particular point of view. Their stories simply can't be told any other way. Second person narrators are often struggling with some element of shame, embarrassment, or regret. They need the distance inherent in the view point to more comfortably access and share their narratives.

I wrote the title story, "Landfall," when I was still in graduate school, and Mike McNally, a professor whom I respect a great deal, had cautioned against using second person point of view. I tried to get that story out any other way, but when I tried to write in third person or more traditional first person, the words just froze up. When you tap into the right point of view, there is a sudden fluency.

JH: You grew up in Big Stone Gap, Virginia. What did you take from your childhood there that has influenced your writing?

HENSLEY: A sense of the power of story. Although I was a child when I lived in Big Stone Gap, I remember how proud the town was of John Fox, Jr., the way *The Trail of the Lonesome Pine* was still performed every summer on an outdoor stage. The story of Liz Taylor's choking on a chicken bone at the Stage Coach Inn was already mythic by the time I was a kid. Even everyday gossip glows in a small town because of the sense of exposure.

An awareness of the beauty in ordinary, useful things (from a quilt to a jar of beans). During my childhood, there was a blossoming sense of the value of folk art. My father was dean at Mountain Empire Community College, and I have visceral memories of the Home Craft Days on the campus each October: the smell of wood smoke, cracklings melting on my tongue, the sound of a fret banjo pulling against my ribs. The festival was usually the weekend of my birthday, so I felt sort of like it was for me that the artists were out weaving and tatting and smithing. I remember an old man, when my mom told him I was five that day, handing me a tiny doll made from corn shuck and bit of blue fabric. It probably sounds like nothing, but it felt almost Eucharistic at the time.

A deep fascination with family systems. People in Appalachia and in the Shenandoah Valley love to track family connections. When we meet someone we often ask something like, "Now who are your people? Are you of the Sandy Bottom clan or the Naked Creek clan?" We are shaped even by what we don't know about our family. I'm very interested in the idea that family secrets can be transmitted generation to generation without ever being explicitly revealed. I think we live around the previous generation's secrets, that our almost telepathic awareness of them shapes our relationships and the decisions we make.

I think most artists carry their childhood landscape like a native language. I am always more comfortable when I can see mountains. My husband, Bob, says that I let out an audible little sigh as soon as we get to Berea—we actually just looked at a house there this afternoon. I went to school in Kansas for two years, and I never got used to so much flat space. I felt like a bird was going to swoop down and get me every time I stepped outside.

I hope the mountain landscape of Conrad's Fork becomes a character itself in *Landfall*, a geographic center like Sherwood Anderson's Winesburg or Wendell Berry's Port William.

JH: You're also a poet, and your collection *Viable* was released last fall. I'm fascinated by all the voices you

embody in those poems—a farm girl who "rise[s] early" to "fight loneliness", a young woman in love watching her "first love" fish, women dealing with pregnancies and miscarriages, as well as grieving mothers and cultural figures. How did all these powerful voices emerge?

HENSLEY: Many of the poems are intensely autobiographical. My husband, who writes nonfiction, loves to joke that I could take the line breaks out of my poems and submit them to *Brevity* [the online flash nonfiction magazine]. Between the birth of my son and daughter, we lost a set of twins in utero, one at six weeks and the other at eleven weeks. I was nearly overcome by the grief—it was as low and out-of-control as I've ever felt. Yet I discovered that miscarriage is a very silent kind of mourning, not something a woman is encouraged to talk about. Eventually, I began writing poems to both crystalize the loss (so many very kind people kept saying that I needed to forget about those babies and move on) and find catharsis.

At some point, I realized I did need to get away from myself. I needed a different vantage point. Then the persona poems emerged. I began writing in the voices of women—mythical, historical, literary—who had lost children in various ways. It helped universalize and relativize my loss.

JH: In "At My Desk, Ten Weeks Pregnant," you write so beautifully of creating, of laboring "each day for perfection," and of the need for rituals. What are some of yours?

HENSLEY: I like to collect things—stones, shells, nests, seed pods—and place them on my desk where they can be easily at hand. Palming a natural object anchors me when I

Hensley's short story collection was published last April.

pause to think. I like to have a warm beverage and just a little background noise. I often write in Purdy's Coffee here in Richmond.

My best writing happens when I can retreat from my life. That probably sounds terrible, but I have lots of people depending on me: two small children, a father-in-law with Alzheimer's, an array of student writers. Sometimes, I'm not good at creating the boundaries necessary to cultivate creative work, so I try to spend at least two weeks a year in a writing residency. My favorite place is Hambidge Center for the Creative Arts and Sciences in Rabun Gap, Georgia. I'm currently working on a novel with several narrative threads, and last time I was at Hambidge, I used ribbons and notecards to literally weave and pin the sequencing to the wall of my studio. Creating a visual element and shifting my spatial distance made huge difference. A residency provides necessary space, both physical and mental. I am able there to find the perfect rhythm for my work: spending an hour reading right after waking, writing for several hours in the morning, hiking in the middle of day, writing though the afternoon, and revising the day's writing after dinner.

JH: Animals are often present in both your short story and poetry collections, whether you are writing about how "girls confused horses with people" in the poem "The Language of Horses" or recording a tag number from a cow's ear in the story "The Sound of Animals." Have animals been important to your life—and by extension, your writing life?

HENSLEY: Absolutely. I grew up on a small farm. We had horses, sheep, chickens, lots of dogs and cats. The first thing I did when I moved away from home for graduate school, even before I bought furniture, was go to the local shelter and adopt a cat. Currently, I live with a Chihuahua, two cats, and two hermit crabs.

I enjoy observing animals with my children. My son, Boyd, in particular, loves to bird watch and creek scramble. Flipping a rock and leaning in with him puts me right back into the childhood mystery of discovery. Last weekend, we went on a group hike in Raven's Run to count stream side salamanders and their eggs.

People are animals. Watching other animals gives us insight into our own social organization, our strengths and weaknesses, our impulses and urges.

JH: You teach at the Bluegrass Writers Studio, the low-residency MFA program at Eastern Kentucky University. What advice do you give writers who are thinking of pursuing an MFA?

HENSLEY: Pursuing an MFA isn't for everyone. It requires a surprising level of discipline and hard work, and it isn't the sort of degree which awards an automatic licensure. It won't guarantee you a book deal or a teaching job. All it guarantees you is a richer writing life. But if that's what you're seeking, there's no better way to immerse yourself in a writing community. If you find yourself writing every week, choosing to write when you could (maybe even should) be doing other things, then it might be time to deepen your writing community. There are alternatives to the MFA—trusted friends who aren't afraid to provide criticism, local writing groups which meet at libraries and literacy centers, conferences and workshops like the Appalachian Writers' Workshop at the Hindman Settlement School. But if you're still seeking more, you might be a great candidate for an MFA program.

The feedback that students get on their manuscripts in a MFA workshop is only a small part of how students grow as writers; they learn as much by critiquing their peers' work. And of course, focused, critical reading of both classic and contemporary texts provides a foundation. MFA programs have evolved in their practicality since I was a student. In the Bluegrass Writers Studio, students learn about the publishing industry and meet with actual editors and agents. They might attend craft leactures on writing a successful grant application or building digital literacy.

I would tell students considering graduate studies in creative writing to research the programs out there carefully and find one that is a good fit. They should consider format (studio/academic, traditional/low-residency), faculty, curriculum, funding, etc., and once they identify possible programs, they should submit their strongest work for the manuscript sample portion of the application. Sometimes it seems like prospective students arrange a manuscript to show breadth when what would really serve their interest is a smaller sample of higher quality work.

I do believe my MFA experience was invaluable. I couldn't have published either of my books without the support I got at Arizona State University. ■

ON LISTENING TO MY FATHER SING

What that song is made of:
ethanol, red dirt, throbbing
fingers, the biggest porch
    you ever seen—

whose father doesn't know
each word to every kind of
blues there ever was?
    Our house got

death letter blues, got broke
down engine blues, got down-
hearted, got travelers' blues:
    lined up, shot

at with the Colt that sored
my shoulder. Son House,
Blind Willie, Mississippi John
    wail around

woodstack, Miss Dolly hums
Jolene's name left of propane
tanks, Robert Johnson behind
    the brick pile.

Twenty-some years, must've
been a hundred times Father
told me all I need is a
    black cat bone

and some mojo; must've been
countless days of backbreaking
work he ran through Muddy's
    dirty bass.

Wiki says a black cat bone
promises good luck, rebirth,
success in love, wards off an
    evil eye.

Guess my father lived a
different life than I made up.
To obtain a black cat bone:
    first catch the

cat, boil it alive—midnight
only—and better be sure you
picked it right. Father says you'd
    hold the bones

up front of a mirror, choose darkest
reflection. See, he hasn't always
been here, making sure I know
    everybody's

got to fall at their crossroad
in order to pray and get back up,
    to seek, take aim.

MORGAN BLALOCK

WHERE THE NEXT POEM IS

On the barest pantry shelf, where preserves crowd
    before summer jams heavy on us.

At the core of the question Mother asks each July:
    Little girl, when did it get so bad?

Inside three years in which I watched your body
    mean things outside of speech.

Second floor of the once-house where the sweetest
    blackest wine is stored in jugs near

bathtub below half roof, filled up half-clear
    with rainwater and ash, with light.

Near the (now collapsed) kilns where William
    Burrell lost both legs in a rockslide

and bled fourteen minutes on the road to C&O
    Hospital in Clifton Forge, 1941.

At the moment Rodney Jones wrote *and this is*
    when it's not language; how I

remember you standing apart from me across
    the white yard grown impossible.

MORGAN BLALOCK

THE POETRY OF PEPPERONI ROLLS

COURTNEY BALESTIER

I need to tell you about pepperoni rolls. But I understand that, as a native West Virginian, I probably have enthusiasm for this dish disproportionate to your knowledge of it, so first I need to explain.

A classic pepperoni roll, one from a place like Home Industry Bakery in Clarksburg, West Virginia, can help us understand the Platonic ideal of the form: yeast bread dough (my grandmother used the same recipe that she used to bake her bread buns) stuffed with satisfying fistfuls of sliced pepperoni or small batons of stick pepperoni and baked. I should also be clear, though, not just about what we're talking about, but about how we're talking about it.

There are words we use when we want to minimize things. We may call something simple or DIY, makeshift or humble or modest. But perhaps the word that minimizes the most, the maximal minimizer, is just. We might say "I just have a question," or, "She's just a stay-at-home mom," or, "It was just a kiss." And it was the just that was on my mind when I was thinking about this piece. Because, for all of the thinking and writing and reading and talking that I've done about Appalachian foodways and about this food in particular, I kept thinking about this eighteen-year-old woman I interviewed once at West Virginia University. When I asked her about this dish—something, now, that's baked in kitchens all over West Virginia, that's sold in cellophane-wrapped six packs in gas stations and grocery stores and dished out at little league fields—when I asked her why we care so much, her answer, basically, was that she didn't.

"It's just bread, pepperoni, and cheese," she said. Now, there is the small matter of her being right. It is just bread and pepperoni. (The cheese is contested; I'm anti, but this is a decision everyone needs to make for herself.) It wasn't a matter of facts, the bone I had to pick with this young lady, but of interpretation. When it comes to the pepperoni roll, as with so much of the food we talk about in Appalachia, the just is the point.

■ ■ ■

The accepted origin story of the pepperoni roll begins in the 1920s with an Italian immigrant named Giuseppe Argiro in Fairmont, West Virginia. There are actually a lot of Italians (or, as they might say, *I-talians*) in West Virginia—so many, in fact, that for a time Italy ran a consulate office in the northern part of the state. Like so many of his countrymen, Giussepe had come to West Virginia to work in the mines. He was no longer a miner when he invented the pepperoni roll, but the problem that he was solving was a miner's problem: the need for a hearty lunch that could sustain a man underground but that he could eat one-handed—a working lunch. Pepperoni and bread was already a popular lunch with Italian miners, and Giuseppe put them together. The pepperoni roll caught on, it grew, it became, as the kids say, a thing, and we still have it today. We have, in West Virginia, declared it our official state food.

The pepperoni roll, really, is a poem: self-contained, complete, economical in every sense of the word.

I continue to find this series of events amazing. Yes, the pepperoni roll is simple, but in the way that an egg looks simple or that a circle looks simple. The pepperoni roll, really, is a poem: self-contained, complete, economical in every sense of the word. And that such a simple food, such bare bones, stone soup, quick-fix food, still thrives today—in restaurants and cook-offs and home kitchens—is extraordinary. Because we glorify a lot of things in American culture, things worthy and unworthy of that attention, but we do not tend to glorify the poor, and we do not tend to glorify the working class. These are concepts very much tied, through reality and rhetoric, to Appalachia, but in general, we Americans do not tend to lavish respect on those who make something out of nothing or on the satisfying meal they've managed to stretch from limited ingredients. If we do, it's usually because we figured out a way to make that meal fancier and get Millennials and food journalists (guilty on both counts) to pay for it. The American dream is about aspiration; it is not about making do. But our man Giuseppe, and the men he was cooking for, they're about both.

Those people all wanted better lives, they wanted good jobs, they wanted to provide for their families, but to achieve all that, they needed lunch. And so Giuseppe, he just figured out how to give it to them.

And now we talk about it. We debate the merits of stick pepperoni versus slice. (Stick.) We talk about Italian bread, French bread, hot pepper cheese, provolone cheese, no cheese. (I've made my feelings clear.) We have, in West Virginia, an entire food economy built around it. My personal favorite actor in this economy, long since gone, was Ray's Bakery, a small storefront near my childhood home. In the summer, on the way to the nerd summer camp that I went to for kids who just wanted to keep reading books, my mom would take me to Ray's, and I would get a donut for breakfast and a pepperoni roll for lunch. We worship this odd food in West Virginia, twinned as it is to our very existence.

■ ■ ■

There's one more story I want to tell you. It's about a gas station chain, called Sheetz, that operates in West Virginia, Pennsylvania and Maryland. Sheetz sells a lot of pepperoni rolls in West Virginia, which it used to source locally from different bakeries around the state. Then, a couple years back,

Sheetz decided to just switch to one central bakery—which, as it happened, was located in North Carolina. People flipped out. They took to Facebook with their anger. The local news covered it. The outcry was so instant and so full-throated that Sheetz actually backed off. It did pick a single supplier, but it was a West Virginian bakery, Home Industry. But my definition of success was not this outcome, great though it was, but a comment left on Sheetz' Facebook page:

You are taking our cultural heritage, making an inauthentic version, and selling it back to us. This is unacceptable.

I thought about this statement a lot. Eventually, it detached itself from food and clung, in my mind, to the word extraction. I thought about all the things that word means in the place I'm from, about all the ways it can and has taken form there. About what extracting this food—just about the only truly unique, idiosyncratic West Virginian food—and reproducing it to West Virginians from the outside, what that can represent to people. What it represented to me.

And then, this simple food became a symbol of something much bigger, especially, for me, at this moment in the region's history and in my history with it. It became a thing that we were ready to stand up for, to fight for. It became something that acknowledged our heritage—without extraction, no pepperoni roll—but that also demanded the right to our own agency in telling that story. It demanded authorship over the chapters of the story yet to be written. It is, perhaps, a lot of pressure to put on a piece of bread, but I choose to believe it can support the weight.

Of course, you probably didn't hear about any of this. The pepperoni roll, it doesn't really travel. Most people outside the state don't know about it. Someone from my hometown married a woman from Memphis who volunteered to make these pepperoni rolls he kept talking about: She bought a huge stick of pepperoni, wrapped it in bread dough and baked what I imagine is the densest pepperoni roll ever pulled from an oven. People have apparently left the state and opened pepperoni roll bakeries elsewhere, but they've tanked. It doesn't translate.

And on this point, I do have to hand it to the young lady who started us off, Ms. Just Bread, Pepperoni and (maybe) Cheese. Because part of the reason is that the pepperoni roll is too "just." It is so simple that it's actually a bit confusing. Anyone who hasn't grown up with it would surely wonder, *Well, why can't I get a sandwich? Why can't I get a slice of pizza? Isn't this just a lesser version of both of those things?* And, in a sense, that person would have a point. I would struggle to explain it to her, this indivisible kernel that is always is at the core of our relationship with food.

It became a thing that we were ready to stand up for, to fight for. It became something that acknowledged our heritage...

I am a West Virginian, but, by fluke of geography and lineage, I am the only West Virginian in my family. My family comes from Appalachia—my grandmother grew up in a coal camp in southwestern Pennsylvania—but I did not grow up in its vernacular of greasy beans and leather britches and cornbread. Which means that, sometimes, I feel as if I snuck into this idea of Appalachia through an open window. But the pepperoni roll. My grandmother made them for me, my mother bought them for me. They're mine.

How does a piece of bread and a stick of meat communicate that message? I have a lot of love for food's ability for metaphor, but they can't. The whole is greater than the sum of the parts. Anyone who does not have the same history of a West Virginian—that same spiritual topography that informs a decision as ridiculous and as vital as a food that we grow up eating and then choose to keep eating—would ultimately come to a place, like a secret door, that they don't even know to understand. What worried me about that young woman at WVU was the fear that we didn't even understand, that we didn't respect it. But those words, *this is unacceptable.* Yes, we do. And honestly, when I was eighteen, I didn't care, either. ■

PASSING THROUGH

I have not written home
In some time, though
There are calls, emails, trips in;
These are the things I do
For my mother, and we are content.

But when I write home, taking ink
To the bodies of trees felled far away,
It is with a vision of my
Windswept, tar-smelling father,
Who always crooks his mouth at my bits of paper,
Feeling love in barely legible lines.

He knows what I know, what
He raised me to know,
That voices, messages over wires—these are not talismans
That comfort when you want to hold
A skinned up hand missing half a fingernail—they do not
Give us root like wood and earth
Or the vibration of a throat nearby.
We do not belong here, we know.

AMY MCCLEESE NICHOLS

CAVE RUN LAKE

At midnight we seek
the lake with no lights
in a canoe so that
we may sit in silver and listen
to the insects sing.

AMY MCCLEESE NICHOLS

TREE WATCHING

Named the false mimosa, the locust's
fine leaves droop in sleep,
allowing rain to feed growth beneath.

Between house lights and other lights of night,
my locust gathers fantasies,
merging with the always-wind down the mountain

that determines what moves and how,
with temperatures that wake skin,
with sounds from land, in air—

leading me in and out of wildernesses.
Real enough, with thorns to not step on in summer,
branches to pick up gingerly in autumn,

I deliberately kill its advancing young,
not needing to build my ships to discover new lands,
grow grapes to brew dreams.

As I hike home down Forge Mountain,
blended to woods, the locust is not;
to communicate, I don't climb,

never made it a point to touch;
but from the roof,
the best of leaf cleaning,

our trunks are most equal,
and immune, safe from tomorrow,
I'm as tall as I can be.

Last to bud and leaf,
last to shed,
faithful to the two true seasons,

the fourth year it exploded—Appalachian desert tree,
royally raining white blossoms
sweet as writing after drought.

Its dryad-harboring trunk,
so canyoned it could be dead,
waits to crush the house from late fall to late spring;

each spring I'm sure that, bored,
it finally will; each fall hope it's evolved
into evergreen, fooling all.

MAREN O. MITCHELL

INTERIOR WITH WINDOW

—Maude Masteller Sockman Brown, 1935

Narrow, curved back stairway
to the children's bedrooms

Wood darkened by generations
of bare feet and sly kittens

No railing, nothing to hold
but a basket of clean socks

On the landing, a window
to the chicken yard, pasture

Three jersey cows and their calves
wander the May meadow

His blue Ford truck kicks up
pebbles and mud, slows then stops

A flurry of children, brighter
from shadows, chirps at his door.

MARCIA HURLOW

BUCKSHOT

RYAN KAUFFMAN

Eddie covered his ears like his father taught him. The mittens felt warm on his ears—the lobes his classmates always said were too big—folded layer of fabric as a barrier against percussion, took his mind off of his stomach ache. Ringing filled his head and cleared out all thoughts but one: his father had lied. The Remington 870 had to be the loudest shotgun ever made.

"Think I got him, boy," his father yelled. His thin handlebar mustache lifted as he smiled and patted Eddie's shoulder with his left hand, naked in the cold. The gun hung from the crook of his right arm. The barrel pointed at the snow-covered ground, gave off a drifting line of smoke as if slowly exhaling. The man had a way of making the boy forget his abnormalities, if only for a moment at a time. Eddie nodded. The buck had only been visible for a split-second before his father gave him the pre-shot wink, and there was no way to tell from this distance if the pellets hit the target. But the last thing he wanted was for his father to take another shot. "Let's go see."

His father picked up the camouflage duffle he used to house his basic hunting tools—hat, gloves, knives and tools for dressing, an unused hand-warmer in case Eddie needed it—and slung it over his shoulder. Snow crunched under foot like peanut shells as they walked toward the small clearing. The woods of southern Kenton County were beautiful this time of year—some baby maples and hickories still clutching their final few leaves, others reaching toward the clouds with empty branches like eager fingers. Everything was shrouded in white, as if nature decided to wipe the canvas clean and start over. The faint scent of pine needles clung to the crisp air.

Eddie didn't know if his Sunday school teacher was right, if there was a God, or if nature was smarter than people gave it credit for. He was certain, however, that there was something more than this, knew it like he knew no player would ever match Rose's record of 4,256 career hits or DiMaggio's 56-game hitting streak. The more he thought about it, the more his stomach churned at the silence of the woods when he closed his eyes. The silence like his own inability to speak.

He wasn't born mute. If he thought hard he could remember a time—a Saturday morning before his mother left, with cartoons playing in the living room—when he'd dangled his feet off the edge of the couch and sang along with her as she made breakfast in the kitchen. Her heels clanked and ticked against the linoleum floor as she scurried about. He asked her for a waffle with extra butter (his favorite then), and she'd answered with "Only if you eat an apple too." But no matter how hard he thought, how tightly he squeezed his eyes shut, he couldn't remember eating the waffle or what cartoon was on or the length of her hair. He could only recall his mother's laugh when he bit into the apple and acted like it was disgusting.

She left on a Thursday afternoon. Whenever Eddie ventured back to that day, he remembered the sky as dark—too dark to be afternoon—the sun's reach blocked by grey clouds that had only begun to produce spittle. The truth was, his father told him on several occasions when the boy had the gall to write out a direct question, that the sky had been cloudless. But the unstable landscape of memory seems to adhere to emotion; it's molded, transmogrified by the raw heat of a

Everything was shrouded in white, as if nature decided to wipe the canvas clean and start over.

blazing furnace powered by sadness or worse, regret. When his mother walked out the door, all Eddie heard was the jingle of her keys. She didn't say where she was going, and the boy didn't say anything. He kept his eyes fixed on the Thursday afternoon spot of *Looney Tunes*—something about a mushroom explosion sending Coyote soaring through the air after another failed attempt to catch Road Runner.

Later—it could have been an hour or five, Eddie didn't know—his father came through the door, his footsteps like thunder on the carpet as he dashed to the boy. He picked Eddie up by the armpits and pulled his son to him. His arms tightened around Eddie like vise grips, as if he wanted the boy to become one with his heaving chest. Everything was wet—his half-tucked flannel shirt, the sprawling whiskers of his auburn beard. The man's legs gave out. Eddie and his father collapsed onto the couch, and Eddie couldn't help but start crying before he knew what had happened. His mother had died, his father told him in sobbing chunks, in a car accident on her way back from the grocery. The accident happened only a mile from their home.

Eddie couldn't force himself to look away from the casket during the funeral—a pale shell, like the porcelain dolls he'd seen little girls his age playing with, that used to be his mother. He thought, as the priest began the service, if he stared long and hard enough, his mother would start breathing again, laughing like she'd just been found in a game of hide-and-seek. But she didn't, even when the casket became pixelated through his tears. Instead, he felt a knot in his stomach. Breaths became more difficult and a grey mass of air—a shadow shaped like a football, tapered at the ends and fat in the middle—seemed to rise from his mother's body. It hovered for only a few seconds before racing to the boy's periphery, where it stayed despite his attempts to turn his head and catch it in full view.

After the funeral, when Eddie tried to tell his father about the shadow, he couldn't. He opened his mouth, formed the words with his tongue and lips, but no sound came from him. The doctors—ten of them, all paid for by his mother's life insurance and double shifts at the factory by his father—were baffled by the sudden inability. His vocal cords, they said, looked fine. It must have been a nerve issue, but his father couldn't find one nerve specialist willing to tinker with anything in the neck of an eight-year old. Or, they speculated, it could be a mental issue, but psychiatrist after psychiatrist said there was nothing wrong with Eddie beyond the obvious trauma of losing a parent. As if to cope, his father began to take the boy hunting.

Walking through a small clearing in the woods after an injured buck three years later, the shadow remained in Eddie's peripheral vision. He struggled to match his father's long strides in the snow as they studied the trees for gouges and holes made by the spreading pellets. The Remington 870 shot .33 caliber 00 buck shells, nine pellets each, at 1,145 feet-per-second. His father had explained that the pellets from the shell would spread out as they traveled toward the target, an inch-per-yard on average. The boy did the math in his head, estimated that the buck had been about twenty-five yards away when his father pulled the trigger, came to the conclusion that the pattern of the pellets would have spread a little over two feet.

Because the shotgun barrel was a circle, it made sense to Eddie that the spread would also be one, but he couldn't help thinking about the expanding circle in terms of right triangles—four of them, connected by their right angles, would create a perfect diamond. He'd been thinking about triangles all week, ever since he learned how to find the length of a side by setting up an equation containing the other two.

Mrs. Ellington had been up at the board. She was a lanky woman, her arms like the legs of a spider jutting from her shirtsleeves. Chalk dust danced around her, caught at her shoulder-length brown hair and wrinkled lapels as she scribbled the day's lesson—Pythagorean Theorem. Other kids Eddie's age wouldn't learn this until next year, but he'd been moved up. When he signed up for the advance math class, he'd overheard a teacher telling his father how smart he was, despite his difficulties. There was always that last part. Grown ups, except for his father, were amazed that someone could be so advanced without the aid of a mother, not to mention talking.

His father, after conferencing with the boy's teachers, would crack jokes about being smarter than them. "I work at a factory and I've always known you were shinier than the average apple," he'd chuckle, or "Maybe all the apples those people eat make 'em slower than those of us who prefer oranges." They were bad jokes, usually revolving around fruit, but Eddie liked them all the same.

His father had mentioned his mother only once in a lighthearted ruse after meeting with teachers. They were in the rusty truck, its engine sputtered with the increased gas. "Like a blue collar gent couldn't raise a smart kid without a woman," he'd said with a huff. His face became expressionless as he ended the sentence. He didn't say anything then, let the silence speak for itself. He reached over and squeezed the boy's shoulder.

Eddie had read ahead in the course's textbook, liked the idea of finding lengths and areas using only numbers—the shape didn't have to be visible for everyone to know it was there. He pretended to write notes, thought about his mother and the shadow in his periphery. Whenever he allowed himself to think about it, to block out everything else but the side of his vision, his stomach would begin to churn. Every once in a while, just for good measure, he would turn his head to the side as quick as he could to try to catch a clear glimpse of it—yet another tick his classmates liked to pick on. But the shadow was elusive, glued outside his focus.

"Edwin Soccumb," Mrs. Ellington said, "Would you please come up front and work through the problem on the board?" The question snapped Eddie out of his reverie, brought reality, the present, back with a sudden jolt. He smiled at his teacher, nodded, and rose from his seat.

As he walked to the front of the class, students sniggered in little cliques. "Why doesn't Dumbo just fly to the board," one student whispered to a huddled group who laughed quietly.

"Yeah," one girl replied, "I pray to Lord Jesus she doesn't ask him to explain the steps as he works through them." But Eddie kept walking, acted like he didn't hear, like the only people in the room were he and Mrs. Ellington. He didn't mean for this to insult the others, but they had grown to expect reactions from their victims.

Eddie picked up a piece of chalk, felt the slick, dry powder dust itself over his fingers, started writing: $x^2 + y^2 = z^2$. He allowed himself to get lost in the equation. What sort of genius must Pythagoras have been to come up with such an easy solution to the problem of finding a right triangle's hypotenuse? Hypotenuse. The word danced at the edge of his tongue like the tang of the first drink of orange juice after brushing his teeth. If he could say one word, perhaps that would be the one. It swooped and twirled, kept the mouth guessing, was theoretical, yet geometric, finite, the kind of word that lets others know, without question, what your mind is capable of.

"Very nice work, Edwin," Mrs. Ellington said as he finished rooting the final answer. "Everyone see how he did that?"

Eddie couldn't help but smile. He'd accomplished something, or at least he felt like he did. The other students nodded their approval to Mrs. Ellington, perfect angels when she was looking or they thought she could hear.

"You may take your seat," she said, motioning towards the desks with one hand. She took up an eraser with the other, her frail, long fingers keeping it from her tiny palm.

And now Eddie was doing the math in his head to find the hypotenuse of one of the diamond triangles. If the pellets formed a circle, then the two known sides would be the same length—the diameter would be 25 inches, making the radius (one side) 12.5 inches. So the equation would look like this: $12.5^2 + 12.5^2 = z^2$; $156.25 + 156.25 = z^2$; $312.5 = z^2$; $z = 17.68$

inches. He nodded to himself, confident with his answer and happy with his keen ability. His father's burly voice snapped him back to the woods.

"There," his father said, pointed out a knick in a tree a few feet away. On the trunk, about five feet from the ground, a gash of the bright flesh shown out from under the bark. "Reckon that could be one of 'em?"

His father had already passed the tree in his search for more explicit signs of carnage. Eddie took in a breath of the pinesap aroma and let it out, felt the astringent tinge he assumed normal people felt when they talked. He studied the gash, the amber sap that slowly worked its way down the trunk, the tree bleeding like his nose did after a bad sinus infection or a run-in with the school bully, Tommy Donovan. He wondered if trees felt pain, if each scrape on bark stung like a paper cut, if they too wished they could talk, if the taller trees around

Eddie took in a breath of the pinesap aroma and let it out, felt the astringent tinge he assumed normal people felt when they talked.

them were in fact their loving parents, if they felt bullied by his father's buck shot.

His last encounter with Tommy came a few weeks earlier in the parking lot after school. He was waiting for his father to pick him up. Buses pulled around the back of the school, away from the bustling post-school traffic of Taylor Mill Road. The sweet, nauseating scent of engine exhaust clouded the air in the small parking lot. Students, from first grade to eighth, stood in their little cliques, laughed at jokes, talked about baseball cards and video games, the anticipation of going on a school-wide fieldtrip to the Cincinnati Zoo in April, once the snow cleared up and the flowers started to bloom. Some of the kids, the ones whose buses still needed to stop by the high school, were in their seats as the buses began to pull out.

Eddie stood by himself, as he always did, at the edge of the school building, where he could peak down the road for a glimpse of his father's beaten GMC Sonoma. His father claimed he'd drive it until he couldn't fix it. And so far, despite what seemed like a weekly breakdown, his father always found a way to keep it running. Eddie thought again about the shadow, how he was sure it was real and not just his imagination. He wondered, as he often had over the past few years, if anyone else was haunted, but he would never write the question down.

"Hey, Dumbo Freak!" The voice came from behind him, a scratchy, high-pitched voice masquerading as a lower register. It wasn't cool to have a high voice if you were a boy—one of the few reasons Eddie didn't mind his inability to speak, he got picked on enough already. He didn't turn at first, hoped if he acted like no one was talking to him they would simply disappear and his father would show up to get him, the Sonoma puttering as it turned into the school's entrance. "Hello, dipshit. I'm talking to you."

"Is he retarded, too?" Another boy chimed in. Eddie judged there were three of them by the laughs. If he listened closely, he could always pick out the subtle distinctions between the vocalizations of others—tiny fluctuations in the sharps and flats of pitch, louder projection from bigger people, a tongue tapping the mouth's pallet to make the "t" sound. One person couldn't sound exactly like another, even if most people agreed it was pretty close. Eddie turned around to meet the boys. "So he was just ignoring us?"

There were three. The biggest of them, Tommy Donovan, a boy with shaggy brown hair, wide shoulders, and needle eyes, stood in the center, flanked by the two that were about Eddie's size. Despite the cold, they'd taken off their coats to show how tough they were. Scrawny little kids—like Eddie—were the only people who needed to be warm. Still, the goose bumps on their arms seemed to say otherwise. They shot glances at each other, acted as if in disbelief. These were not the kind of people who could just be ignored, or so they obviously thought. They were important, and so was their need to feel important.

"Is that it, scab," Tommy said, "you think you're better than us?" He stepped closer, showed how much taller and wider he was than the others. Eddie looked him straight in the eye. "Oh what, you got somethin' to say, dumbass? Go ahead, then." The other boys laughed, joked about him being tongue-tied or speechless. Eddie felt heat build inside him, started in his stomach, radiated upward through his neck. Time seemed to slow down—he could swear he could pinpoint the exact location of a nearby fly suspended in mid-flap as it zipped ten feet away. A bus shifted into drive. The teacher on bus lot duty was chatting with a driver, probably speculating on the chances of more snow. Eddie's father's clanking truck was still nowhere to be seen or heard.

"Holy shit! I think he's gonna cry!" The three started laughing, chanting "cry baby" over and over like a mantra. Eddie lifted his hand, scrunched it into a fist, extended his middle finger the way he'd seen his father do when another car pulled in front of them. If he could speak, perhaps he would have chosen to say the words that always accompanied the gesture.

"Real cute," Tommy said. He stepped forward, grabbed Eddie by the shirt and pulled back his right arm. Eddie closed his eyes, didn't want to see the fist hurtling toward his face, saw only the shadow rising from his mother's porcelain body before it shifted to the side.

Eddie cupped a mitted hand over his eye with the memory. He'd had a black eye for almost a week after the confrontation. He stared at the sap trailing down the tree from the gash—amber syrup creeping through the cracked bark like a slow-motion rendering of water in a canal. He pulled the mitten off his free hand with his teeth, the fabric scratchy on his tongue as he touched the sap with his fingers. It was sticky, created a level of friction that his thumb could barely overcome when he tried to rub it. It seemed warm on his skin, as if the tree pumped the sap through a regulated circulatory system like humans. Then again, his fingers may have just been unusually cold.

"Over here, Son," his father said. The man waved his hand through the air like swatting at a swarm of flies, bounced up and down on his toes. Eddie made his way through the brush—between leafless branches, over little snow-burned ferns and bushes – felt the knot in his stomach grow when he saw splotches of dark red melting a staggering trail through white. "A four-pointer!" His father's smile widened. The shadow danced in the boy's periphery as he looked at the buck's antlers, felt as though he'd double over from nausea, counted the points. He looked at his father, held up six fingers, pointed at the tiny buds his father must have missed. "Well, looky there," his father said. "Six it is. Nice eye, son!"

The man had made many such comments over the past few years—he never missed an opportunity to give Eddie a feeling of accomplishment. But the boy wondered, in times like these, if his father had really been mistaken or if it was all a ruse. The man was notorious for his keen mechanical eye. Whether amongst the countless conveyor belts and pressing machines at the factory or tinkering with a neighbor's car for a few extra dollars, he wasn't one to miss any of the details. And yet, like with the points, this seemed to happen all the time when it was just the boy and his father. But did this make Eddie feel any less good when his father praised him? No. Instead, Eddie only felt trust and the respect that stems from it. The more he thought about it, the prouder he felt to have the ability to pick up on the tiny details his father left for him to discover.

Some things, though, his father still did without the help of the boy. After Eddie's confrontation with Tommy Donovan, his father sputtered into the parking lot. His shoulders sagged from the weight of a demanding day at the factory and his hands were stained black from the machine grease. His smile dropped when he saw the puffed eye of his son. Eddie had gotten enough black eyes and split lips that his father knew what had happened.

"You okay?" He waited for Eddie to nod, swallowed the boy in a tight hug, and walked him to the truck. "I'll be right back."

Eddie watched as his father stormed across the parking lot toward the teacher on bus lot duty. The man's steps were heavy, but quick on the blacktop—in a way, it seemed like his father was stomping toward the teacher. His father started yelling, threw his hands around in large gestures as he put the teacher in his place. When he was finished, he shook his head as he made his way back to the truck. He snapped the driver's side door open and stepped in.

"No discipline," he muttered. The man turned to his son, grimaced at the sight of swelling, patted Eddie on the shoulder. "Was this Tommy's work?" When Eddie nodded, his father shook his head and shifted the truck into drive. "It's time we take care of this."

The truck clanked up Taylor Mill hill, whistled around the turns. Eddie wondered if the alternator belt would need to be replaced—one of the first things his father checked when the truck started making groaning noises—and what his father was going to do. He'd never seen the man so angry. His father's knuckles were white on the steering wheel as he drove, his mouth turned down at the corners as if to emulate the curve of his mustache. The shadow danced in Eddie's periphery, teased at darting to the center of his vision, but remained where it was.

They turned onto Ishmael Road, bounced up and down on gravel, passed a group of sycamores shedding leaves. To the right, Pineview Trailer Park sprawled into the surrounding woods—its concrete basketball court dusted with snow, the hoops void of nets. Trailers with rusted siding and shredded screen doors stood to either side, shiny Camaros and GT Mustangs parked in their lots. It didn't make sense to Eddie why a person would want to own a car that was more expensive

His father's knuckles were white on the steering wheel as he drove, his mouth turned down at the corners...

than his home. He thought about his own house—the brick ranch his father constantly cleaned, the quarter-inch yard during the summer, the beaten GMC truck sitting outside a sparkling garage. That was what made sense. His father pulled the truck over in front of a doublewide, shifted into park, and turned the key with a flick.

"Here we are," he said. He swung his door opened and stepped out with one foot, swung back and shot a glance at his son. "You want to come with me?" Eddie shook his head. He felt safe in the truck, the cabin comfortably warm from the drive. His father nodded and patted Eddie's leg. "I'll be in view the whole time."

Eddie watched as his father rounded the front of the truck and walked toward the trailer. He bounded up the steps of the wooden front porch two at a time, shook his hands as if to free them of dust, and knocked on the door. Eddie rolled the window down to hear the upcoming conversation—the crank took both arms to wheel.

"Get your ass out here, Tim!" His father's voice was booming, the way a lion's roar must sound coming from the waving-wheat edge of an African plain. The door opened, revealing Tim Donovan in cut-up jeans and a sleeveless shirt. The man's black chest hair protruded from the neck of his shirt, a kind of compensation for the receding hair on his head. He was only slightly taller than Tommy—an adult version—with broad linebacker shoulders and a layer of middle-aged fat around his previously muscular arms and stomach.

"What the fuck is this ..." Eddie's father grabbed the man by the shirt with both hands, pulled him through the doorway and slammed him against the side of the trailer.

"We've got a problem, Tim," his father said. "My boy's been getting picked on by your little dipshit." The man's eyes were wide with surprise, hands hanging opened at his sides. "It's going to stop, got it? If it doesn't, I'm going to come back here and finish this conversation." Eddie's father slammed the man against the trailer again. "Now nod your head so I know you understand." Tim nodded. "Good. Enjoy the rest of your day." When his father got back in the truck, he shifted into drive, pulled away from the trailer, turned back onto Ishmael Road, and looked over at Eddie. "That boy won't be bothering you anymore, Son," he said, reaching over to pat the boy's shoulder. And Eddie believed him.

Since then, Tommy had kept his distance. The other boys seemed to have lost interest as well—followers rarely act without a leader. Now, Eddie leaned against a tree as his father opened a bag with tools for field dressing the animal—a few knives, each with its own purpose though the boy couldn't remember what they were, and a corkscrew contraption known as a "Butt-Out", which was used to dislodge the colon from the carcass. There was something wrong, something different. After his father's first cut, the smell of the buck's insides permeated the air, stung Eddie's nostrils, but that wasn't it. Red pooled under the carcass, burned its way through the snow like sulfuric acid through aluminum, but that wasn't it either. The shadow—it had moved from his periphery and was watching them, moving around Eddie and his father in a circular motion without touching the ground.

Eddie felt pressure in his chest, vise-grips tightening on his heart. His lungs took in less air with each breath. This, he thought, was what death felt like. He thought it without thinking, suddenly knew it, had always known it. His father pulled out the buck's stomach, tossed it to the side. He'd told the boy on more than one occasion that some animal would come along and make a meal of it. A thin line of steam swirled upwards from the deer's exposed innards, waltzed to the tune of some inaudible song.

The twirling steam reminded Eddie of the fire at their camp last night—the way the embers crackled and smoked as he cooked hotdogs over the flame. He breathed in the mesquite smell given off by the wet wood as it burned. His father had brought a baggy filled with marshmallows, graham crackers, and miniature Hershey bars for s'mores. Snow, large flakes the size of silver dollars, began falling as Eddie held the marshmallows over the fire until they caught flame. He and his father both liked them burnt. Eddie couldn't help but think about his mother—how she'd liked her marshmallows to be only slightly warm, not burnt in the least; how she'd hated the woods and camping. It seemed he was more like his father than he'd thought. He pulled the burning mallows from the fire, blew out the flames with a puff, wrenched them from the skinny branch with pair graham crackers, a Hershey bar on the bottom, and handed one to his father.

"This may be the best one I've ever eaten," his father said, the "b's" muffled through a full mouth of sugar. Eddie smiled, felt good about his ability to cook over an open flame. He snuggled up next to his father. They ate their s'mores in silence. Then, they sat there, his father's arm around the boy's shoulders, watching the fire and snow flakes until Eddie fell asleep—safe, connected, content.

"Now the fun part," his father said, pulling Eddie back to the present. The man winked and grinned with the words. His father's left hand disappeared into the carcass, his right hand screwing the "Butt-Out" in. The colon, and what remained of the animal's intestines, came out in one swift pull. He tossed it aside, careful not to mix it with the stomach. He turned to his son, motioned toward the two distinct piles with a shining hooked knife that contrasted with his red-soaked hand, and said, "Different critters'll come by for different parts. The colon's for the birds."

Eddie wondered if his father was right. Did wolves instinctively know not to touch the birds' meal? For a second, the idea of order was soothing. The knot in his stomach eased and air reached down into his lungs, burned as his chest expanded with the full breath. His father pried the animal open and inspected the edible organs—heart, liver, kidneys—using the hooked blade to loosen them from the casing fibers. Eddie knew the animal was dead, that it could no longer feel what was happening, but he could swear the heart fluttered when he looked at it. The knot in his stomach returned. That's when he saw it—the shadow moved to the center of his vision for the first time since his mother's funeral, hovered over the buck for a moment, then dispersed in all directions too fast to see where it went. ■

NORTHERN MISSISSIPPI

Brother, do you remember? All those years ago?

How sticky pinecones crunched and crackled
when we stole into the silent woods,
the moon above like a coin of butter melting
into the frosty misty midnight air,

How our frozen fingers clutched flashlights
as we followed the grownups with their rifles,
you dashed ahead but I wasn't far behind,
the heat of adventure pulsing hard in our chests,

How we scoured the bony treetops and then:
the telltale glint and crack of a shot,
the coonhound's echoing howling haunting
that dew-bejeweled meadow we pelted across,

How blood welled from our hands and cheeks
as we plunged into thorny brambles,
and the carcass lay stiff by the maple's trunk
as we stood, our breath kindling heat, immortal—

How it took all our strength to lift it by the tail,
its death reeking of copper and shit, moonshine
sloshing among the men, sips even burning our lips
as the pine trees bowed to forgive us our silence.

BEN GRONER III

ACCIDENTS

ALICE MARTIN

Rhoda gripped the tough, pockmarked skin of the willow's sturdy chest. It seemed like she'd been there forever, her feet asleep, sitting on the aluminum stand that was strapped against the trunk of the tree. Like most things, it felt unstable beneath her.

Her father, Dixon, sat on an identical treestand set up in the old oak beside her, his shoulder pressed to the tree as if he were trying to force his way inside it. His rifle was tucked under his arm, facing the clearing before him. She never took one of the rifles he offered her. She preferred to sit and watch.

"Don't move," he warned her. He didn't need to. She knew the consequences of shifting, snapping, breaking. She knew the consequences of making a move.

They'd been there since the early morning but the sun had risen an hour ago and the cool night had sunk into the cushion of mud beneath the tree. Her breath marked the air with mist and she looked down at the ground below her. Perhaps the earth was cold and it needed something warm, a sip of her body's heat. Perhaps it would suck her under, tree and all.

There was a snap in the woods around them. Her father lifted his rifle, readjusting his weight on the trunk. She looked over at the oak beside her, how it grew slanted, as if the years of her father leaning against it had slowly pushed it over. All these years he used this oak tree as his post. But she preferred to sit beneath the grandmother willow, where he said he couldn't hunt because the branches would block his shot. She watched him hunt from beneath the rustling tears of leaves, beneath the eyes of the wary weeper.

A deer stepped out of the brush in front of their trees. It was young but strong. A buck. The rack on top of his head was small still, the antlers like fingertips, just beginning to reach at the sky. A man at the beginning of his life. Rhoda could see the young, untested muscles in his shoulders under his short fur, drawn tight.

Dixon's shoulders tensed, tendons pulling taut against the skin on his neck. He raised the rifle. *Shut your eyes now,* he used to say when he first brought her here. He stopped warning her long ago. Perhaps he thought she knew when to shut them now that she was seventeen. But she'd never learned.

The deer's head pivoted in jerks. Its globe eyes stared at the woods around it. Its eyes were so close she could see the reflection of the willow's falling branches.

The jerking stopped as the globes landed on the barrel of Dixon's rifle, peeking out from behind the trunk of his tree, the eye of a dead animal. She waited for the deer to bolt, to spring to life.

"Dad," she said, more an exhale than a word.

Dixon never turned. His eyes stared into the deer's. She pressed her chapped lips together. There it was, she thought. A promise. A promise that he was someone to trust.

They stared at each other, the deer and Dixon, until he pulled the trigger and the shot exploded through the crisp air like a fist busting through a thin sheet of ice.

Dixon lowered the gun and turned to smile at her. His eyes still hadn't blinked since they'd seen the deer. He gave her a thumbs up. She buried her head into the tree's skin and waited for the mud to swallow her whole.

■ ■ ■

Once Dixon loaded the deer into the back of the Jeep Wrangler, his hunting car, he gave his daughter a hand into the passenger seat. His hands were scratchy with thin deer hairs, like a barber's hand after a haircut.

"It's dead, right, Dad?" she asked. The Jeep started beneath her.

He rubbed his close-shorn beard with one hand and kept the other gripped around the steering wheel.

"What kind of question is that?" he said. "'Course it's dead."

She nodded.

"What kind of question is that, Rhoda?"

She shrugged. "Its eyes are still open."

"That don't mean nothing," he said.

I know, she thought. Then she said, "It means somethin."

When Dixon said nothing, Rhoda added, "Promise it's dead, Dad?"

Dixon's eyes didn't even flicker. "'Course I promise."

Even now, after years of Dixon breaking his promises to her, a part of Rhoda was still comforted by these words.

The car tumbled across dirt until they reached a main road, paved over with cracked asphalt. The deer in the back was already filling the car with a salty, cold scent. Dixon had tossed its body into the back of the Wrangler, where he'd ripped up the carpet years ago so the blood from his kills wouldn't stain it, linger there, fester.

Dixon rubbed his hands on his muddied jeans as they drove. Those were his hunting jeans, just as the hat he wore with the dull green color and rabbit silhouette was his hunting hat. The flannel button-down and the bright orange, sleeveless

The deer in the back was already filling the car with a salty, cold scent.

vest were his hunting clothes. His tall-necked, mud-choked boots were his hunting boots. And his lined, frozen face, his lips peeled from the cold, his eyes glazed over, that was his hunting face.

Rhoda slipped her feet out of her hunting boots, a pair that had once been her brother Otis's, and tugged off her woolen socks, damp with cold sweat. She put her feet over the rasping heating vent. It coughed out small bursts of warmth that smelled of exhaust and tar. Her toes prickled as the cold ran up her feet and through her legs. She stared at the chipping yellow paint on her toenails.

"Who did that to your toes?" Dixon asked.

"Mama," she said. She reached down and began chipping at it again.

He grunted.

When Rhoda was younger, she never had nail polish on her toes. Instead, the skin beneath her nails would be black and blue, the skin around them red and cracked from the cold. Dirt caked beneath nails torn short, toes perpetually curled from being shoved into too-small hiking boots. These were the feet of a girl whose father took her hunting every Saturday. Even after he left Mama he would come, without invitation, bouncing and shaking down the gravel driveway to their white-washed rancher, the Jeep grunting and rolling to a stop behind the porridge-colored Sedan Mama'd bought after he left.

Rhoda still remembered how that sound would wake her on cold Saturday mornings, how she would push her feet into her old boots and tuck in her double-layered sweatpants before the rumbling engine cut off. He wouldn't ring the doorbell because he didn't want to see Mama. They hadn't spoken outside of the divorce proceedings since everything with Otis happened.

Dixon would stand with his back resting against the muddied Jeep, wearing all his best hunting gear, until Rhoda would tumble down the front stairs in her ill-fitting attire. She'd run to give him a hug and he would kiss her thin, white-blonde hair through the unlit cigarette tucked between his lips. Then he would lift her into the Jeep and light his cigarette as he walked around to the driver's seat.

While they drove away, Rhoda imagined Mama lying awake in bed, thinking she could smell his cigarette smoke.

■■■

When Rhoda started high school three years ago, after everything that happened with Otis, Dixon had stopped coming most Saturdays, even though every time he came he promised he'd be there next weekend. These days he only came occasionally. She would wake up anyway, the ghost grumble of the Jeep's motor jarring her senses. Mama made bacon on the Saturday mornings Dixon didn't come, the burning bacon grease singeing the air. His absence gave her a smug self-assurance, an air of achieving something. Rhoda played along; she felt bad for her.

As his visits lessened, Rhoda would sometimes have dreams of Dixon out in the woods alone in his hunting clothes. He would whistle the same lullaby he'd sung to Otis when they were both young, coaxing creatures out of their beds with sweet promises. Then, beneath the willow that seemed to breathe, he would shoot them.

■ ■ ■

Rhoda's toes were completely warm now and she tucked them beneath her and pressed her hands to the vents instead. Her cheeks were flushed with aching heat. Beside her, Dixon was lighting up a cigarette as he tried to balance the steering wheel between his knees. Behind her, the deer lay dead.

"D'you want me to get that?" Rhoda asked. She nodded to the lighter.

"Yeah," Dixon said around the cigarette. He reclaimed the steering wheel as she took his tarnished Zippo lighter.

He leaned toward her, his bloodshot eyes still on the road, as she flipped open the lighter and slid her thumb across the wheel. A few empty *thwicks* and the flame jumped to life with the sharp, lingering smell of oily lighter fluid. In the dull light of the early morning, the fire was a stroke of color. It illuminated Dixon's graying beard and the redness at the tip of his lumbering nose. His lips cupped the cigarette as he took his first drag and leaned back. Rhoda leaned forward, catching the last whiff of his nicotine-sweet breath.

"You still in school?" he asked. He rubbed his red eyes with one hand. They looked irritated.

"Yeah," Rhoda said. She flipped the Zippo lighter open, then closed again.

He squinted at her in the crooked rearview mirror and adjusted its angle, leaving a muddy thumb smudge on the glass. "Got a boyfriend?"

Rhoda shifted closer to her window. "No," she said.

He sucked on his cigarette like a straw and grunted something.

"Your Mama want you staying away from them or something?"

Rhoda remembered nights long ago when Dixon would be gone for days and Mama would lock herself in her room, crying.

She shrugged. "You want me staying away from them?"

"Hell, I don't care what you do."

He scratched at his eyes again. The stray deer hairs on his hands seemed to be irritating them.

Rhoda picked at the loose, chapped skin on her lips. In a year, she would be out of high school. Mama wanted her to go to the local community college but all of her friends were going to big universities out of state. She wouldn't tell Dixon. He wouldn't care if she did anything. After Otis, he didn't care what anyone did.

She wasn't sure he'd even cared what anyone did before what happened with Otis. Rhoda remembered nights long ago when Dixon would be gone for days and Mama would lock herself in her room, crying. One of these evenings, when Rhoda was twelve, Otis sat on the front porch steps with a lit cigarette between his teeth, scuffing his shoes on the concrete. He looked up and smiled as Rhoda sat down beside him.

"You're worrying again," he said.

She tugged on the hem of her shorts. They were getting too small for her.

"That bastard'll be back," Otis said. He held the cigarette out between his forefinger and thumb as if to examine it. Rhoda knew Dixon must have bought them for him because Mama never would have let Otis have one. "He always comes back."

"He always *says* he'll be back," Rhoda said. Her voice was so soft that it nearly drowned in the burr of the cicadas.

Otis put the cigarette in his mouth and his hands on his knees. He turned to look at her with mock-anger. "You don't trust me, Rhoda?"

She smiled. "I trust you."

"You don't trust our daddy?" He lifted an eyebrow.

She thought of Dixon's sweet words, his strong, smooth voice, his soft eyes.

"I trust our daddy," she said. But she couldn't decide if she really did, or if she just wanted to.

Otis grinned around the cigarette and pulled her into his side. "Good," he said. "Sometimes, Mama don't trust him. But as long as we trust him, he'll always come back."

Rhoda wished these words were true, just like she wished Dixon had kept all the promises he made to them. She wished he'd remembered her birthday was last week. She wished he'd come to her ballet recital, after she'd made him write it down so he'd remember. She wished he would quit smoking like he said he would. And later, she would wish he was there when Otis needed him most.

■ ■ ■

In the Jeep, Rhoda wanted to reach for the radio dials but she knew better than to turn on music since what happened to Otis. Mama and Dixon had first fallen in love over music and they'd told Otis they'd named him after Otis Redding. Otis used to tell Rhoda they must've conceived him while listening to Otis Redding on the Jeep's radio. She could never tell if he was joking or actually guessing. Mama always said she knew he was going to be a boy before he came out. She said he was always her Otis.

Rhoda and Otis were both accidents, but after *the* accident, neither Mama nor Dixon would ever say so again. They didn't seem like accidents after what happened to Otis on the highway. Not after a truck made a U-turn without looking and slammed his grey Volvo station wagon—the only car Mama would let him have because of its reputation for being a safe, sturdy car—into a safety rail. Not after Otis showed up in the hospital, mostly dead already. Not after Mama called Dixon, who was off missing again. Not after Dixon never came until a month later, when Otis was long dead.

Otis had a pack of Marlboro's on him even though he'd told Mama he'd quit. Rhoda remembered hearing that after they'd been given his personal effects. It'd stuck in her mind, like the string of chewing gum plastered to the underside of Otis's worn shoes.

■ ■ ■

They were close to the gravel driveway now, Rhoda noticed. Only a few more miles and it would slide into view over the slight crest of a hill.

Dixon tossed the butt of his cigarette out the window of the Jeep, sending it flying backward with a trail of ashes behind it. It was just after the cigarette had flown out the window and hit the ground yards behind them that the Jeep gave a jerk.

Rhoda looked over at Dixon. His red eyes were still staring into the sun. They were blazing yellow with the reflected light.

Another jerk and Rhoda grabbed the ledge of her open window.

"Dad, stop it," she said. "I can drive if you want."

"It's just the car," he said. "It's just old."

Rhoda looked toward the horizon again. The crest of the hill was coming into view. A gravel road off to the right. Suddenly, all she wanted was to be home and away from the muddied car that smelled of sweet smoke and sweat and blood. She wanted so badly to please Dixon. But she couldn't make false promises like he could. If she could, everything would be easier. If she could forget how much she wanted to trust him and finally open her mouth to say something to him, everything would be easier.

Another jerk and suddenly Rhoda knew what it was. She looked behind her in time to see the deer in the backseat give a mighty kick. Its eyes were wide as globes again, misted over but flashing wildly in the fiery light of the sun. Its hind legs kicked squarely into the back of Dixon's seat, pushing him forward. His foot slammed onto the gas pedal as his head pounded into the steering wheel. It left a smear of blood.

Rhoda tried to grasp the dashboard as the car spun beyond the road and away from the gravel escape, toward a muddied ditch. For a moment, the car flew through the air with the world spinning around it, as if lost in gravity, before its front bumper smashed into the base of a pine tree. Browning pine needles cascaded down onto the crunched and smoking hood. The airbag on the driver's side exploded from the steering wheel, pushing Dixon's unconscious body against the back of his seat before deflating, like a chest exhaling after a gasp.

Grasping the windowsill with one hand and her strangling seatbelt with the other, Rhoda stared at Dixon's face, which lay relaxed and passive. His jowls hung slack, the stubble on his cheeks pressed against the airbag's once bulging, now emaciated, form. If it weren't for the blood streaking down his face from his hairline, he would look as if he were asleep against a pillow.

In the back seat, the deer was still thrashing, rocking the Wrangler from side to side and tossing Rhoda against her seatbelt and back into her seat. Her neck was beginning to sore from whiplash. The smell of burning rubber and exhaust stung her nose and mouth.

Rhoda took a few, rapid breaths, squeezing her eyes shut against the banging around her. The deer huffed heavy, breathy grunts from the backseat. In her head, the world was still spinning, just as it had been only a few seconds before. She replayed that moment when she thought she was going to die. When she thought she would be free.

Her eyes jolted open when the deer smashed his back leg against the window in the back door. The glass cracked and the deer thrashed again, its leg punching through the window completely this time, the glass bursting into a waterfall of shards. Rhoda looked back at the deer again and met its gaze. Its eyes were just as glazed over as before, but its body twisted and turned as it tried to find its legs. Its breath rushed in and out in quick, desperate snorts from its muzzle. Its still-small rack of antlers raked at the back of their seats, slashing holes in the fabric like exaggerated scratches left behind from desperate, grasping fingers.

Its eyes connected with Rhoda's.

Rhoda unsnapped her seatbelt, and tried to open her passenger side door but found that it was crunched in slightly and stuck. She twisted in her seat until her feet were against the door and she kicked at it, cried out in frustration, and finally forced it open, tumbling onto the ground in her haste. The cold mud squeezed between her fingers. She got to her feet and ran to the back of the Jeep. A few pieces of scratched glass remained in the window but the rest had fallen to the ground or lay on top of the deer's hind legs. Through the window frame she could see the deer still kicking for its life.

She would have liked to tell it Dixon didn't mean to hurt it.

She would have liked to tell it Dixon had done everything he could to make sure it was dead before he piled it into the back of his Jeep.

But these things were lies. And Rhoda wasn't going to say one thing and do anything. In fact, Rhoda wasn't going to say anything at all.

Taking a deep breath, Rhoda opened the back door of the Jeep and jumped away from the car. In a second, the deer clambered to its twig-thin legs. Then, it shot out the back of the Jeep and bounded up the steep slope of the ditch, leaping across the road and out of sight.

Rhoda stood in the stillness for a moment, letting her bare toes feel the mud beneath them and listening to her own breath over the sound of the breathless engine steaming. She had the salty aftertaste of copper blood on the back of her tongue and for a second she wasn't sure if it was her own or the aftertaste of the deer's scent. She wondered how long the deer would last in the woods alone, the bullet wound in its side and the cuts from the broken window in its legs. At least it would die free.

A moment later, a groan came from the front seat as Dixon struggled against the seatbelt trapping him in his seat. Rhoda closed her eyes, waiting to feel some kind of relief that he was awake, that he was alive. But none came.

"Rhoda?" he said, his voice guttural.

But Rhoda was already trekking up the edge of the muddy ditch and toward the road. The gravel driveway wasn't far ahead. She would walk the rest of the way on her own. ■

RUTS

I dream gone home about ruts,
an old road we don't use
where the rain wash has worn
from trails shallow gullies
that curve as they twin down
the hillside, crushed exposed
sandstone, yellow layered,
grey gravel big as boys' fists,
"erosion" a word I
don't know to say, like "drought,"
when a green unmown ridge,
an overgrown ribbon
of grass, holds a barefoot
soft path for a hard-ankled
boy near new property
lines hemming in, hemming in.

THOMAS ALAN HOLMES

ASHAMED AT WHAT I NEED

Roy always welcomes when I arrive (again)
bathed in Saturday manure, mud and sweat,
knowing already each inch of a cabin filled
with the essential—the wood stove, the spring pump,
the bookcase proud with well-used ancient texts/
the covered porch where he rests to watch
the world approach.

Inside above the mantle are tinted and faded pictures.
John Henry and his famous pet groundhog;
Sam in military surprising uniform kneeling
to fit the frame. To the side, as if still alive,
Father Sherman smiles at mountain grandkids
dressed in Easter clean. All suggest this
family remains self-sufficient and whole,

and actions say it all—together they work forever
shelving jellies, wine, apples in the root cellar,
and care for guests, for ham and beans
and corn bread are always magically ready.
And predictable—the Christmas cactus will bloom
red after Thanksgiving—in March the pie-tin
tomato seedlings will crowd the window sill.

Usually I go to Roy, but this morning he is on
my new stained redwood deck, hat in hand,
smelling of work, returning what he sees as mine.
Inside my huge house he breathes spring
eagerness with knowledge of how the birds
scramble to build nests. At my dining room table
he is animated drinking from his favorite

red/white mug. I am disheveled, coated in
night oil as he speaks of strawberries, firewood,
chickens, creasy greens in the creek. I recoil at my
stagnant stench, too rich for him to understand.
As his goodness fills the room, I cringe at
the flash and decoration so shiny, at all
that I require to go on.

MARK VOGEL

LITTLE SHOP OF WRITING

C. WILLIAMS

A few years ago I had to find a place to write. I'm not the kind to sit at home in the quiet. It gives me what I call *Monkey Mind.* I am a social creature, raised in chaos and noise and visual distractions.

I wanted a studio. A tiny one where I could have the option of quiet, but still watch the flow of humanity stroll by my window. Being someone who craves contact with others, I had to pick a spot where I didn't feel isolated, but not be distracted by coffeeshop gossip and unhinged toddlers. I wanted to create my own silent movie. Make up stories about the people walking by. Play soundtracks. Come up with complex scenarios about the lives of complete strangers.

I'm writing fiction, so this is what I love to do.

For years, and another career, I struggled with the idea of writing. I did some all my life. Wrote a play in the third grade that was a mash-up of Robin Hood and Goldilocks. Bow and arrows, bears and a shotgun. It was a hit. Ran for a week during morning snack break. I knew I was going to be a writer.

Then I hit a dry streak. I wrote intermittently in junior high study hall, high school pep rallies, on crowed beaches and cafes in college. I required people in a humming hive to dive into the place of myself to write. All the images I ever saw of writers were sitting in a dark attic office or walking alone by the ocean, wind in their hair. Thinking. Alone. No one else seemed to dream of an author photo taken on the streets of New Orleans during Mardi Gras.

I was screwed.

Then in 2009, I was lucky enough to be included in my first week long writing event in the haven of the Appalachian Writers' Workshop at the Hindman Settlement School. The experience spoiled me with the kind inclusion and generosity the writers there extended to the odd new girl among them. Beginners and bestselling authors worked shoulder to shoulder, intent with serious craft offerings and lots of love. It was perfect. It was five days of a communal kindness and inspiration that one could use a dose of every day, especially the hard ones.

I wanted to come back home and try to share a taste of this feeling.

In December 2012, I moved into a writing space that's in an enclave of stores in East Nashville called the Shoppes on Fatherland. It's a popular area; lots of foot traffic. I wanted my studio to be a kind of humane trap for other lone writers wondering the streets of Nashville, looking for shelter. Then I did something un-writerly.

I worked with the door open. Literally.

A shop-front window space allowed for public display of my wild, awkward leap from visual design to writer. Who knew how it should work, certainly not me. But it seemed important to expose myself to the many questions people have about what the place is about when they stumble across my studio. It helps me clarify what I mean to do. I had to really consider the why and how of dedicating this sort of time and money just to sit and make stuff up. The only answer I know is that this special little hut keeps a place for me, and I keep coming back to write. It has a spirit, a soul, so it keeps me accountable. Especially when I want to give up.

It has a spirit, a soul, so it keeps me accountable. Especially when I want to give up.

To be straight about it, this place is a kind of bait. It was in hope of finding a way to connect with as many people as possible over the solitary journey of writing. Some days there's a steady stream of friends and strangers who walk in the door trying to figure out what the heck I'm doing writing in a what looks like a store. Most like the space and many feel like there is something here they need and want. The ones who do, return. We sit and write and talk and write some more.

That's what it does. That's it.

Others just stick their heads in to ask where they can get waffles and hot chicken.

I love having company in my studio, but lately I find I need more time to myself. It's hard to believe. But the day comes when you must pull into your work, lock your door, and dig deeper. Go for the place that tips the scale toward the soul-rending depth we need as multi-sensory creatures. Try to become that writer. That narrow and deep cut is only done by oneself, day after day, one blind step of faith after the other. Alone.

If there is one thing that terrifies someone who thrives on contact with other humans, it's the idea of isolation. I'm looking for a balance between camaraderie and seclusion.

Alone. Together.

The other reason I picked a storefront as a studio was to make a point about the realistic efforts and the unheralded hard work of writers. The idea was to plant the seed in the minds of shoppers on the street, that art requires showing up every damn day and doing the work. Even when you feel like you're stumbling and failing, you have to drag your ass to your room and do the work. Our culture has forgotten this. So this is a kind of shameless, subtle Performance Art.

You cannot make art if you think it's a hobby.

The general populace doesn't understand the dedication it takes to produce 300-plus pages of a book they consider entertaining enough to pay for and take to the beach. Some eager soul is divinely happy to sit alone pulling the story from their body, one fragile string at a time.

Those things don't fall out of a vending machine. Not yet.

The spot we pick is important. You're gonna need a portal. In my tiny 200 square-foot writing studio, I have a ridiculously soft and enveloping leather chair. I call her Carmen. She was sitting in a friend's curated furniture shop and it was love at first sight. She had me at Friends' Discount.

A lovely place to sit was important because I am not by nature, one who sits. When I'm writing here, my body dissolves. It absorbs the physical me and lets my mind float out on a tether where I can be with the people, places and creatures that are kind enough to speak to that phantom of myself. It's the one part of me that simply asks, "Who are you?" It knows to shut up and listen. If I think too much about how my legs are sore from a workout, or my eye hurts because… allergies, I drop the link. Physical awareness is a distraction I will cave to every time. I love my chair, Carmen the hypnotist.

She's my favorite drug.

For a lot of wonderful years, I've worked in the TV/film industry as Production Designer and Art Director. Still do, but less. This job means you're responsible for imagining, designing and then bringing forth a 3-D world that allows a real place where people and their stories can exist. I have learned to be a World Builder.

When I found the right space for my writing studio, it was natural for me to put a lot of thought and effort into the world where I planned to develop my skills to become a better writer. Every color, every object, each smell I bring to this personal place has a reason and a job in helping me achieve this. The music I listen to is specific on some days, completely random on other days to keep my brain flexible and curious.

Of all the specific objects I surround myself with, one stands out because it has been with me most of my life. It came to me the winter I turned five. I was playing under the huge cedar tree that spread over our backyard. It was my spot. It was magnificent.

Trigger Warning: As a child, I had invisible friends.

My pals favored visiting me under the big cedar. They sometimes made suggestions about the little chairs and beds I made for fairies out of willow twigs. This visit, the girl one handed over a beautiful blue rock that looked like a lumpy Earth, about the size of a nice biscuit. She said this would be the last visit I'd remember. She said they were awfully sorry, but I was growing up. The rock was to keep me from forgetting… something.

I have to have the little blue rock on my desk. Sometimes I try to remember why.

If you are looking for your own writing space, I'm pretty sure it can be anywhere that puts you in the frame of mind that keeps you coming back, every day. It should push you, open you up, but offer safe harbor. It should make you mourn for it on days you cannot be there within its arms. Find a place that feels like new love for an old flame, or first glance at a familiar stranger. Every time I walk in my studio door, the first thing I say is "Hello." I can tell it's glad to see me.

It's our thing.

I have met many wonderful people by leaving my door open on good weather days, fellow travelers on this path and others whose curiosity was struck by the idea of an actual writing space.

"Do you actually write in here?" many have asked.

"Yes," I say, "I'm trying."

Some stay to chat and gift me with personal insights on the miracle of human experience. Others politely back out the door, move on round the corner for waffles and hot chicken.

Can't say I blame them. It's hard work up in here. ■

DAUGHTERS IN WONDERLAND

I used to pick the trash up out of the ditch
on Patterson road in Smiths Grove. It was there
I saw him spit out his window, bent can
at my feet. As soon as I cleaned up one thing
there was a new paper bag, a new bottle.
People couldn't wait to throw something away
on the red clay dirt of our name and pasture.
My father said fences perfected land.
He said they should look like they've always been there.
Maybe God always wanted these divisions.
My father hungered for borders just like I
hungered for a word for my secret earth:
a land of caves and sinkholes, my heart the most
extensive cave system on earth. I know
my father's right about fences and borders.
Imagine the settlers faces as they crossed
over the natural bridge into Kentucky:
they must have whispered it was wonderland.
Who could blame them for not sharing what they'd found.
Have you seen this? Have you ever seen this?
And then, retreating into what they'd found
it was asked among them, how to keep others out?

TASHA COTTER

BOOK REVIEW

Carrie Mullins. *Night Garden*. Lexington, Ky.: Old Cove Press, 2016. 241 pages. Softcover. $16.00.

Reviewed by Donna M. Crow

The aptly titled *Night Garden* by Carrie Mullins is a virtual seedbed of characters— characters whose virtues are hidden in the shadows of their circumstances, fertilized by an apathetic economy, isolated by geographic region, and choked out by drugs and depravity.

The novel is narrated in the voice of Marie, a seventeen-year-old protagonist coming of age in a place with very little light, forced to bloom where she is planted. Through a series of poor choices, Marie navigates dysfunctional relationships, grief, abuse and teen pregnancy while searching for solid ground where she can grow.

Mullins's use of metaphor and tone are evident in the opening scene: "Marie, her brother Shane, and their teacher Ms. Anglin got out of the car…They had to go around the wet mud pit in the middle of the road, had to walk up into the woods a little bit, over rocks they couldn't see for dead leaves, and then back down onto the wide path, until the shadows they'd been watching became people…"

The shadows became people. This is much more than a description. These "shadows" surround Marie throughout the novel and become the rocks and dead leaves that Marie must climb over to survive with any sense of self. Her brother having an affair with his teacher is simply a matter of fact, only one of many facts that may surprise the reader yet seem second nature to the narrator. Everyone in the narrator's life has a distorted view of reality and Marie seems to have adapted the same, accepting her lot as normal. She doesn't view herself as a victim which makes her a refreshing yet unreliable protagonist. She narrates her story almost as if she's numb. In this way Mullins delivers the harsh truth of the region in which her characters inhabit without judgment, hyperbole or apology. We are given the facts through the narrator's eyes and left to make our own assessment.

Mullins's command of language is enviable. She is stealthy, quiet, her pacing deliberate. Using words such as dark and shadow and phrases such as "climbing over rocks hidden by dead leaves," Mullins prepares the ground for a garden that blooms in the night.

This debut novel is a beautiful garden nonetheless tended with care and watered with hope. Hers is a well-honed craft, paying particular attention to detail and technicality. Rich in symbolism as well as sense of place, this Appalachian based novel is character driven, highly literary, and yet also a page turner. It does not fall into the trap of shock value and stereotypes to push the narrative forward as might catch the attention of the masses. Yet Mullins does not shy away from the underbelly of the region. Her characters are real, raw, fully drawn human beings, both vulnerable and tough, whose choices, though sometimes limited by circumstance, render lasting consequences. Her narrative is forthright but compassionate as she lends us her microscope to view the inner workings of a tight knit, albeit dysfunctional, community. Though set in Appalachia it is much more than a regional tale, it is a story of the current human condition and thus has universal appeal. *Night Garden* is a jewel. ■

SEAFARERS

Some say Saint Brendan traveled
from Ireland to West Virginia
long before Columbus ever set sail.
Perhaps that's why the Criel and
Grave Creek burial mounds of the
Adena bear a ghostly resemblance
to the Neolithic earthen domes of
Brú na Bóinne. The solstice sun
kisses Ogham petroglyphs in the
Tug River Valley on its overseas
journey to the triskel-carved cover
stone of Newgrange, soft beams of
light illuminating the passage tomb
through the corbel arch, bouncing
between bookended emeralds, the
green-hued mountains and waters
of Glen Ferris and Glendalough.

V.C. MCCABE

THE PARTING GLASS

So fill to me the parting glass
Good night and joy be with you all
—Traditional

In Harper's Ferry, where the town
square's antiquated shops still
smoke after desecration by fire,
two rivers converge, crowned by
Blue Ridge Mountains, crossed by
steel and timber railroad bridges.
The Appalachian Trail imbibes
the Potomac panorama before
its trek into northern wilderness
and transatlantic ocean immersion
end at the Irish coast, sliding up
the Slieve League cliffs of Donegal
and down the Sperrin Mountains of
Tyrone to grab a Guinness in an
Ulster pub, toasting every glorious
mountain climbed between the
rivers Shenandoah and Shannon.

V.C. MCCABE

CONTRIBUTORS

Courtney Balestier is a James Beard-nominated writer whose work has appeared in the *New Yorker* online, *Oxford American, Lucky Peach,* and *Cornbread Nation 7: The Best of Southern Food Writing.* "The Poetry of Pepperoni Rolls" is adapted from a talk given at the 2016 Appalachian Food Summit in Berea, Kentucky.

Morgan Blalock graduated from Hollins University in Roanoke, Virginia, but now lives in South Park, Colorado. You can find her work in *CutBank, The Adroit Journal, Collision,* and *Prairie Margins.*

Tasha Cotter is the author of the poetry collections *Some Churches, That Bird Your Heart,* and *Girl in the Cave.* Winner of the 2015 Delphi Poetry Series, her work has appeared in journals such as *Contrary Magazine, NANO fiction,* and *Booth.* A contributor to *Women in Clothes, The Poets on Growth Anthology,* and the *2017 Poet's Market,* she makes her home in Lexington, Kentucky.

Michael Croley was born in the foothills of the Appalachians in Corbin, Kentucky. He won an NEA Fellowship in Literature in 2016, as well as an Ohio Arts Council Individual Excellence Award. Croley's work has appeared in *Lit Hub, Narrative, Kenyon Review Online, The Paris Review Daily, Blackbird, Virginia Quarterly Review, The Southern Review, Fourth Genre,* and the Cleveland *Plain-Dealer.* He teaches writing at Denison University in Granville, Ohio.

Donna M. Crow lives in Irvine, Kentucky, on her family farm. She writes fiction, creative nonfiction, and poetry. Her nonfiction has received the Emma Bell Miles Award for essay, the Wilma Dykeman Award, and the Betty Gabeheart Prize. Her work has appeared in *The Louisville Review, Kudzu, Now and Then, Literary Leo,* and *The Minnetonka Review.* She received her MFA in creative nonfiction from Spalding University.

Ben Groner III of Nashville, Tennessee, is the recipient of Texas A&M University's 2014 Gordone Award for undergraduate poetry, and has had work published in *Third Wednesday, Texas Poetry Calendar,* and *One Sentence Poems.*

Leah Hampton's work has appeared most recently in *North Carolina Literary Review* and *McSweeney's Internet Tendency*. She has won North Carolina's James Hurst and Doris Betts Prizes for her fiction. She teaches English at A-B Tech College in Asheville.

Thomas Alan Holmes, a member of the East Tennessee State University English faculty, lives in Johnson City. His work has appeared in *Louisiana Literature, Valparaiso Poetry Review, Appalachian Heritage, The Connecticut Review, North American Review, Pine Mountain Sand & Gravel, Still: The Journal,* and *The Southern Poetry Anthology Volume VI: Tennessee.*

Marcia L. Hurlow is the author of six collections of poetry. Her most recent chapbook, *Brushstrokes on Water*, was published by Finishing Line Press in December 2016, and her full-length collection, *Anomie*, won the Edges Prize at WordTech. Her poems have appeared in various journals, including *Poetry, Poetry Northwest, Nimrod, Poetry Wales, Stand, Miramar, The Iconoclast, Hawaii Pacific Review, Malahat Review,* and *Mudfish.*

Ryan Kauffman is an associate editor for *Passages North* and an instructor at Northern Michigan University. His previous work has appeared in *Rathalla Review, The Rumpus,* and *Word Riot.*

Jay Kidd's poetry has appeared in a number of publications including *The Bellevue Literary Review, Ruminate Magazine, Burningword, The Florida Review* and *Atlanta Review.* A four-time Pushcart Prize nominee, he was the winner of *Ruminate*'s McCabe Prize for Poetry in 2013, and was a 2015 winner of *Atlanta Review*'s International Poetry Competition.

Bill King is a 1990 graduate of the M.A. program in Creative Writing at the University of Georgia and has taught literature and creative writing at Davis & Elkins College in Elkins, West Virginia, for the past twenty years. His work has appeared and is forthcoming in several journals and anthologies, including *Kestrel, Appalachian Heritage, Still: The Journal, The Southern Poetry Anthology,* and *A Narrow Fellow: Journal of Poetry.*

George Ella Lyon is the current Kentucky Poet Laureate. Her most recent books include *Many-Storied House: Poems, Boats Float!* and *What Forest Knows* (picture books), and *Voices from the March on Washington,* a collection of poetry for young adults co-written with J. Patrick Lewis. A native of Harlan County, Kentucky, she makes her living as a freelance writer and teacher based in Lexington.

Alice Martin received her BA in English and Creative Writing from the University of North Carolina at Chapel Hill, where she received the Max Steele Prize in Fiction Writing. She has worked as an intern for *Carolina Quarterly,* Press 53, Algonquin Books, and Folio Literary Management. Her work has appeared in *Carolina Quarterly* and *Cellar Door.* She now does editorial work at Writers House Literary Agency in New York City.

V.C. McCabe is a West Virginia poet, writer, and music journalist whose work has appeared, or is forthcoming, in *Poet Lore, Prairie Schooner, Spillway, The Galway Review, Appalachian Journal, The Charleston Gazette-Mail* newspaper, and many other journals. She resides with her husband in a book-filled cottage on the bank of Elk River. Her website is vcmccabe.com.

Maren O. Mitchell's poems have appeared in *Iodine Poetry Journal, The Lake (UK), Appalachian Heritage, The South Carolina Review, Hotel Amerika, Southern Humanities Review, The Classical Outlook, Town Creek Poetry, The Journal of Kentucky Studies, Appalachian Journal,* and elsewhere. Her work is forthcoming in *Hotel Amerika, Chiron Review,* and *Poetry East.* She lives with her husband in the mountains of Georgia.

Amy McCleese Nichols grew up in Flemingsburg, Kentucky, and remains invested in the places and experiences of her home region. Her poetry explores the interplay of the sacred and the everyday in these settings. Nichols is a doctoral candidate in Rhetoric and Composition and the 2016 recipient of the University of Louisville Creative Writing Award for Poetry. Her work has also appeared in the "Appalachia Under Thirty" issue of *Pine Mountain Sand and Gravel.*

Kristian Thacker was born in West Virginia and grew up in the shade of a steep hillside in the Ohio River Valley where light was fleeting.

After being given a camera by his grandmother, he started taking photographs and drew inspiration from those he saw in *Rolling Stone, National Geographic,* and *Time*. He is still learning, and hopes that he will always be learning.

Gail Tyson shares a log cabin in the Cherokee National Forest, East Tennessee with her husband and border collie. She has published poetry in *America, Kindred, Naugatuck River Review, Pilgrimage,* and *Still: The Journal.*

Mark Vogel has published short stories in *Cities and Roads, Knight Literary Journal, Whimperbang, SN Review,* and *Our Stories*. His poetry has appeared in *Poetry Midwest, English Journal, Cape Rock, Dark Sky, Cold Mountain Review, Broken Bridge Review,* and other journals. He is currently Professor of English at Appalachian State University in Boone, North Carolina, and directs the Appalachian Writing Project.

C. Williams's fiction has appeared in *The Louisville Review* and *Appalachian Heritage*. When not writing, she works as a production designer for sets in film, television, and commercials. She lives on the eastside of Nashville, Tennessee, the best neighborhood in the known world.

Warner James Wood studies poetry at the University of Michigan Helen Zell Writers' Program (MFA). He graduated from Harvard Univesity with a degree in Human Evolutionary Biology. He was born and raised in Blue Ridge, Georgia.